thrive

LIVING A SELF-HEALED LIFE

thrive

LIVING A SELF-HEALED LIFE

VALARIE BUDAYR

 AUDREYPRESS

Audrey Press
P.O. Box 6113
Maryville, TN 37803

For information about special discounts for bulk purchases, please contact Audrey Press Special Sales at info@audreypress.com

Cover and interior design by Andy Meaden meadencreative.com
Photography by Peter Ellzey

Manufactured in the United States of America
10 9 8 7 6 5 4 3 2 1
Library of Congress Control Number: 2021949405

978-1-936426-31-7 ISBN for the print book
978-1-936426-32-4 ISBN for the e-book

ACKNOWLEDGMENTS

To my village.

My tribe at Audrey Press, you motivate me and inspire me every day, and I am forever grateful that I get to create beautiful books with you. It takes a village to make a book, and I couldn't do it without any of you.

To Becky Flansburg, a ginormous amount of thanks for all of your help and guidance on this book. Thank you for walking alongside me throughout this journey and in business the past 11 years. My life is greatly blessed because of you.

To Mallory Adamson, thank you for your guidance and deep insights during the writing of this book. Thank you as always for bringing your talents to this project. In my heart and mind you are and will always be the best editor ever.

A moment of gratefulness to those who offered tools and held space for my healing: Aaron Rose, Dr. Peter Fisk, Daisy Lee, Sara Colquhoun, and Dr. Joe Dispenza.

I honor all of my teachers, guides, and Ancestors.

Lastly and most importantly, I honor the love and blessings I receive from my wonderful family Zaina, Miriam, and Omar, my dearest friends.

DEDICATION

This book is lovingly dedicated to YOU who is reading *Thrive*.

Sending much encouragement and holding space for your healing journey.

CONTENTS

NOTE FROM THE AUTHOR

We heal in community.

Self-healing is not a journey in which we walk alone. If you are under the care of medical and/or psychological professionals, please continue your plan of care. The message of this book is to empower the reader to assume their active and essential role in their healing journey. In no way is this author suggesting that anyone should discontinue any treatment that is recommended by the medical or psychological community. Everything that follows is meant to be an addition and enhancement to your life, not a substitute.

With that, I wish you, in all ways, be well.

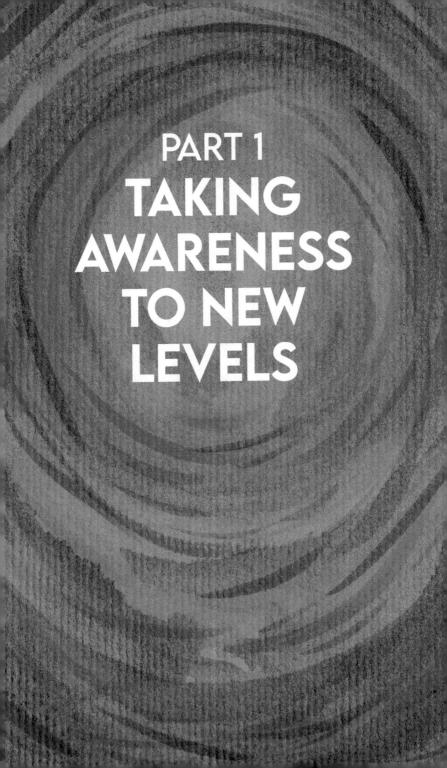

PART 1
TAKING AWARENESS TO NEW LEVELS

INTRODUCTION

The hero of this story is *you*.

The hero of your quest to healing can only be you. It is not your doctor or your therapist or your yoga instructor or your best friend or your partner or *anyone else*. Although all of these people play a very important part in your journey, *you* hold the power to grant yourself the whole and vibrant life that you want and deserve.

I am writing to you because, as a culture, we have been taught always to look **outside** of ourselves for healing. If you are feeling sick, you put your physical health in the hands of an M.D. and seek relief through prescription medications. If your emotions are off-balance, you put your mental health in the hands of a therapist. Now, I am not saying you should not access these services when you need them; what I am saying is that, even within traditional medical and psychological practices, you are always THE foundational element in your healing. We are not taught this in Western culture. We are always seeking someone who can cure us or fix us, but the truth is everything you need to heal already exists inside of you.

What I am about to share with you are things that you can implement and practice, adapting them to your individual needs to make a profound difference in the quality of your physical, mental, and spiritual experience. What I want for each and every one of you who picks up this book is true healing, a restoration to wholeness. Underneath all your trauma responses exists a complete and whole human being. You don't need to be fixed. You don't need to be more. You just need to be wholly and vibrantly you. In this book, I will guide you and teach you about the areas of Breath, Movement, Sound, and Meditation and how they can work to deeply connect you to your essence and help you to manifest a self-healed life.

I want to start by asking you a question: *Are you Thriving or Surviving?*

In the evening, are you exhausted and relieved just to have "made it through" another day? Are you perpetually stressed or worried? If so, then you are living in a state of *Surviving*.

There is a huge difference between Surviving and Thriving. *Survive* means to continue to live or exist, especially under hardship and despite danger.

The characteristics of Surviving are:

- Experiencing your life from a place of lack, not abundance

- Choosing the path of least resistance so you won't create friction

- Reacting to what is thrown at you instead of making conscious choices for yourself

- Blaming others for your circumstances

- Feeling stuck

- Feeling inauthentic

- Fearing failure and believing failure means that things are going in a wrong direction

Thrive means to prosper, be fortunate or successful, grow or develop vigorously, and flourish. When you have reached that point when your daily routine includes the things that nourish your soul, lift your vibrations, and clear your mind, *then* your Surviving will shift to *Thriving*.

The characteristics of Thriving are:

- A sense of safety

- A sense of self-worth through compassion

- Trust in yourself and others

- Centeredness: coming into alignment with your authentic self

- Acceptance

- Being able to observe things from a place of non-judgment

- Gratitude

- Creating from a place of abundance

- Owning our pain and healing instead of projecting our pain onto others

- Embracing mistakes and failures as learning opportunities

Many of us keep tending to the status quo survival mode because it has become a life habit. Even an unhappy routine can feel comfortable and familiar after a time. The second reason many are stuck in survival mode is FEAR.

Fortunately, there are several tools, many of which we will talk about here in this book, that can help you transform fear, trauma, pain, and stress into healing, so you can live your one big and precious life to the fullest.

I am inviting you to enjoy these practices with me. Each of us comes to this practice with no degrees, awards, financial successes (or un-successes), or accreditations.

We come together as equals and just as we are, doing the best that we can at that moment. For example, if you come into this practice with asthma, allergies, or lung damage, you will be coming into a breathing practice in different ways on different days. There will be days when your breath flows easily and days when the pollen count is off the charts. Just do your personal best at that moment, and it will always be enough.

My wish for you is to live a life where your chronic illness, dis-ease, or turmoil is not at the forefront of your mind every day. My plan for you is to begin a journey of self-love and self-compassion that works to honor all facets of your life.

Let us begin this new journey to self-healing together.

CHAPTER 1
WHEN THE BOTTOM FELL OUT OF MY BOX

Merriam-Webster Definition of Bottom Drops/Falls Out: "a phrase used for something that suddenly fails or becomes unable to continue in a normal and effective way."

Self-healing snuck up on me like a freight train if I'm perfectly honest. I was one of those people who spent a whole lot of years (and even more money) trying the latest quick-fix self-help remedies, searching for a home that I never really had and that elusive "thing" that would make me feel "okay" once and for all! But, much to my recurring devastation, my efforts to rise above the angst and darkness in my life sputtered and failed more times than I could count. I knew I was wounded. I knew I was broken. But how to take the first step to true and continued healing eluded me.

The day that I had the epiphany that I could no longer continue the way I had been, I was collapsed on my couch in exhaustion. I was overcome by feelings that I could no longer carry the heavy emotional and mental load that had been weighing me down for years. I felt like I was deep inside an overloaded box and the bottom seam was about to give way. My "seams" were bulging and threatening to spill my distress and emotional wounds all over the place, and I knew I didn't have the strength to clean up the mess.

When the bottom fell out of my box, it was in the slow, plodding, continuous way that dribbled out fragments of my life with every step I took. One by one, the contents of the box dropped and left a breadcrumb trail of "stuff" in my wake. Soon, I was losing my balance while trying to clutch the box and still grab at the things that were leaking out. Finally, in defeat and frustration, I had no choice but to give up and just let it go.

"Life whispers to you all the time. It whispers, and if you don't get the whisper, the whisper gets louder. If you don't get the whisper when it gets louder, I call it like a little pebble — a little thump — upside the head. The pebble or the thump upside the head usually means it's gone into a problem. If you don't pay attention to the problem, the pebble then becomes like a brick. The brick upside your head is a crisis, and if you don't pay attention to the brick upside your head, the crisis turns into a disaster and the whole house — brick wall — comes falling down."

— OPRAH WINFREY

Lying there on that couch, I had to wonder, when did the whispers get louder for me?

Did I ignore the whispers, chalking it all up to stress and age, continuing to plow blindly forward through life?

Was it when I could physically feel the front of my brain quivering inside my head? Was it when my body began to break down to the point that I was having trouble walking? Did my body, frustrated that my brain and heart wouldn't pay attention to my emotional crisis, **make** me pause when my knee swelled up painfully for no apparent reason?

Did the whispers turn into to a *"Pay attention, Valarie!"* shout when I could no longer recognize my own voice in my own head? Did the awakening attempt to intercept when I saw that I was spending the majority of my waking hours worrying about making others happy?

I'm sure all the signs and whispers were there over the years; I was just too caught in the swirl of mental and emotional trauma to hear them.

Before my Bottom of the Box Falling Out moment, I was like a hamster on a wheel. I spent my days powering forward with an "I'm fine! Everything is fine!' mentality, even though things were far from *fine*. The darkness of loneliness, neglect, and feeling "not enough" was creeping its way into every fiber of my being.

Looking back on my most challenging years, I can see that these whispers were calling to me, but I wasn't hearing them. I **knew** that I was wounded and broken. I just didn't know how to verbalize that pain, much less how to deal with it or make it stop.

Years later, the clarity I needed to make the changes in my life hit me hard and fast. The day the bottom fell completely out of my box began as a calm, quiet, and uneventful morning. Then, there was the smallest shift in perception, but it was big enough to knock my rose-colored glasses off for the first time. Suddenly, with crystal clarity, I saw things so completely differently. In that moment, I saw that my greatest desire was to simply hear my own voice. To hear the Old Me, the Wonderful Me that still existed but was buried so deep inside of Current Me she was close to being lost forever.

She was buried deep, but I knew She was in there.

To give a bit of context to my personal journey, allow me to share with you that it took a while for me to realize that my emotional trauma dated back to childhood and the tenuous relationship I had had with my mother. That moment of clarity came while I was listening to a Sounds True Summit on narcissism. The host spoke about identifying the abuse of a narcissist and how the effects and severe damage of a narcissist's torment can unknowingly shift our whole perception of self and life. As I listened, I ran the gamut of feelings from anger and sadness to remorse and resentment because I could identify with every bit of what he was saying.

I finally felt heard. I felt validated.

In those five days of the summit, it was like having my blinders ripped off. There was a profound awakening in my heart and mind, and I realized that I needed to fulfill what my mother could not do for herself.

I could acknowledge that there was a lot of pain, chaos, and turmoil in my birth family, but we always attributed that to my mother being an alcoholic. It was now that I realized that she, too, was in so much unprocessed trauma that she turned to alcohol and needed to control everyone to try and soothe her own wounds.

The following week I made an appointment with a psychiatrist who specializes in healing from narcissism, and I asked her how do I **fix the narcissists** in my life? She revealed to me that there **isn't** a cure for narcissists because part of that disorder is not having a conscience. Their inability to register the pain they cause others stems from the pattern of the narcissist's need to numb their own pain. She said the only person I could help was **myself**, and she advised me to get far away from the narcissists in my life. So I did. I physically moved myself to a new place and a new life.

What I received on that fall October day was a Wake-up Call. And it was a big one. When I arrived at the moment of the wall crumbling down and the seams of my hypothetical box giving way, I woke up to what matters most to me.

These realizations often come when you lose something, or nearly lose something, that you treasure. Wake-up calls teach us how to live more gratefully, how to live with our hearts wide open, how to remember and lean into the experience of life that we're longing for.

Wake-up calls are often painful. They shock us into remembering what we would be well-served to remember **all** the time. Maybe you can remember a wake-up call in your life. Illness, losing loved ones, divorce, addiction, violence, a devastating accident, loss of use of your limbs, financial collapse, betrayal, or community crisis. I know that there are many of you who have had a wake-up call due to grief and loss. These wake-up calls send shock waves through our lives and do just that: **wake us up.**

We're blessed that most of these shock waves are temporary and we're able to get back what we've lost. These are the "wipe the slate clean" moments when we, because of the wake-up-call, can dive into this deeper appreciation of all that we do have.

When we focus on what we do have, instead of what we don't, there is always more to celebrate.

Wake-up calls wake us up into this revelation. They remind us of the things we need to pull closer to us and hug tight—the people, situations, and things that make our hearts sing. Through this newfound clarity, we realize that we can no longer take things for granted. Sometimes facing a loss, or near loss, is all it takes to give us insight into what our priorities are, a fresh knowing on what we treasure.

Imagine being on the side of the road after you've just avoided a near-collision. After you've slid, spun, or swerved, you find yourself on the shoulder of the road thinking, *Oh My God, I'm alive.* The profound thankfulness that the worst didn't happen hits you harder than any car wreck could have.

Following my wake-up call and subsequent move, I came to terms with the fact that I couldn't blame the people, life situations, and conditions that, over a lifetime, had left me in a traumatic state. The enemy was *my* coping techniques. I, like so many, was caught in the trap of spending too much time in my head. I was looking out into the world for validation or for cues on where I needed to go next.

Do you ever find your mind ruminating at high-speed on questions like, "Is this all there is for me?" or "Are people happy with me?" I did. Constantly.

All of this looking outward for comfort and validation leaves us feeling isolated, alone, tired, and sometimes depressed when we can't find the answers we crave externally. What I learned, and what I want to share with you, is that those answers you're looking for are not "out there somewhere." They are very close to you. They know you are looking for them, and they are trying to speak to you. You only have to learn to receive them.

For many years, I recognized a perpetual sense of longing inside me. This deep loneliness and a desire—no, a nostalgia—for belonging. The word "nostalgia" means "pain for home." I felt as if I were in exile, longing for distant shores. I have literally traveled the globe searching for "home," belonging, and my place in the world. It took me decades to realize that home had always been waiting for me. I call my healing a "coming home" process, because, as I showed up daily for my inner-work and inner healing practices, I realized that I was having a homecoming, not to a place but to myself.

I realized the more we search high and low and far and wide for our well-being and happiness, the farther we veer away from what we are searching for. Through my practices of breath, movement, meditation, and sound, I found my sense of belonging, and my "pain for home" subsided. Just like a migrating bird that uses the earth's magnetic field to fly thousands of miles and arrive home to its nest in the same tree year after year, each one of us holds that navigation system to find our way back home and to be welcomed there. The journey home starts with bringing awareness back to our body.

CHAPTER 2
OUR WISE BODY
AND FRIEND

Our bodies are designed to handle anything life can throw at us. To navigate this challenging world we live in, we create coping strategies. This includes using things like food, alcohol, or shopping to mask difficult emotions and thoughts. At this point in our journey, many of us are facing the reality that the coping mechanisms we thought were working for us, helping us deal with life, are actually harmful habits that need to be rewired in our brains. For example, some people have everything in their lives organized to the nth degree. Hyper-scheduling is a deeper indication of our discomfort with being alone ourselves. Others of us are out of balance in the opposite way, spending our money in ways that lead us into financial struggles or filling our homes with clutter as a result of "retail therapy." Our outward disarray reflects an inner state of *doing*, which we will talk more about later in this chapter.

Whatever your unhealthy coping strategy, it is rooted in your brain. Did you know that our bodies can become addicted to the chemicals our brains produce? If you live in a constant state of stress and drama, your brain will disperse an excess of stress hormones, like cortisol, and your body will begin to crave these substances. Then, in order to get more of what your body is craving, you will (subconsciously) create more stressful situations in your life. This, in itself, is a symptom of Survival Mode. The stress, although harmful to us, feels familiar and safe. When we are addicted to stress, a peaceful life feels strange and threatening.

As we begin this new journey to Thrive instead of Survive, we need to rewire our brains to welcome a state of Being instead of a state of constantly Doing. When we do this, our body ceases to crave the negative energy that has been fueling us thus far.

Entering a new state of Being doesn't involve throwing money at a problem, ruminating on hypothetical worst-case scenarios in our minds, or waking up filled with dread about what the new day will bring.

It will involve simple practices that connect our bodies and minds: Breath, Sound, Movement, and Meditation.

When our minds and bodies are connected, that's when we can access the wisdom we already have built into us, which will lead us to self-healing.

3 STEPS TO UNLOCK THE WISDOM OF YOUR BODY

1. Return to Your Body as Home and Stop Looking Outside of Yourself for Healing
2. Release and Transform Your Negative Programming
3. Connect with Life Source Energy

Before we begin studying the 3 Steps to Unlock the Wisdom of the Body, we need to address the pervasive myth that blocks us from accessing it in the first place.

THE #1 MISCONCEPTION

We have learned to view everything as separate. Human beings tend to be disconnected from our bodies, because we see it as a separate thing. There's me, and there's my body. In this scenario, we incorrectly believe that we are our mind. Our mind is so busy thinking that we perceive it as ruling everything, especially the body. When we think of ourselves this way, there are mental and emotional ramifications of that disconnect.

SOME OF THE SYMPTOMS OF OUR MINDS BEING SEPARATE FROM OUR BODIES ARE:

- Feeling inner loneliness, separation, conflict, and a general disease and unhappiness about life.

- Feeling stressed and mentally busy. Your mind may be ruminating all the time, hyper-focusing on one big problem, or needing to have drama in your life.

- Feeling unsettled and always looking for a home base or someplace to call home.

- LACK of feeling. There is a disconnection from your heart and feelings. You are not "feeling all the feels."

- Self-loathing. There is a lack of self-respect and self-love, and you do not feel whole and complete. This usually leads to us unconsciously permitting others to treat us the way we treat ourselves.

- Feeling disempowered. We feel deprived of voice, power, authority, or influence, which, in turn, makes us feel weak, ineffectual, or unimportant.

Humans typically don't like feeling emotional pain, so we avoid it at all costs and stay in a place of stress, anger, and unhappiness because it feels familiar to us. Even though these symptoms cause us a great deal of suffering and are harmful to our overall well-being, too often we accept them because, over time, these negative feelings have become familiar to us. In fact, we can become so used to our stress, anger, and unhappiness that we reject any opportunity to make changes that would improve our emotional and mental state. The idea of changing the status quo is scarier than living with the disconnect. But to access self-healing, we all must be willing to spend some time reconnecting our minds to our bodies and *breathing through the discomfort.*

STEP #1
RETURN HOME TO YOUR BODY

When you return to your body, you can access the power and wisdom already programmed into your body. When mind and body are connected, you will feel an inner sense of home.

Your own body is the source for health, healing, and happiness. Throughout the ages, we've been taught that the keys to happiness exist outside our bodies, i.e. I need a great job so I can buy a big house and raise 2.5 children, and that is what will make me happy. This simply isn't the case.

You, and only you, can access and master your energy to improve all the functions of your mind, body, and heart in order to realize your full potential. No matter what others tell you, you must look inside yourself for the solutions, not outside.

You can discover the healing power and wisdom within you and practice it to heal your life. You are the only one who can do this. No one can do it for you.

WHEN YOUR MIND AND BODY ARE CONNECTED:

- You feel an inner wholeness.

- You feel at home and settled inside yourself and your body.

- You are "comfortable in your own skin."

- You feel self-compassion and self-love.

- You discover the wisdom of your body and your heart.

- You connect to the power within.

- You discover inner joy, bliss, and peace.

- You discover your authentic nature.

I want to be clear: This whole and authentic self that you become when your mind and body are in sync is not the same as the outward "shiny" self you want the world to see. Your inward "real self" might look a little dull and messy right now, but I can promise you that the more you embrace that person, the more she will shine in the world.

STEP #2
RELEASE AND TRANSFER YOUR NEGATIVE PROGRAMMING

Have you ever noticed how our modern-day culture focuses on the negative and tends to acknowledge the bad before the good? Each one of us has a set of behaviors based on this programming. Even asking someone how they are these days is likely to result in 10 minutes of listening to how horrible their life is right now.

Instead of greeting people with "Hi, how are you," I've gotten into the habit of asking, *"Tell me what's good with you today?"*

It's not that I don't care about people's struggles, but I think it's important to encourage others to acknowledge the good in their lives as well.

TYPES OF NEGATIVE PROGRAMMING:

- Emotional: fear, anxiety, anger, depression, trauma
- Mental: negative thinking, limiting thinking, judgment, blaming, disempowerment, disbelief, denial

These various types and forms of negative programming reduce us to our smallest state of being, and we go through life feeling constricted or in a state of contraction.

Our minds always want to figure things out, so they are in a constant state of busyness. Breath, sound, movement, and meditation clear the mind, but they also help it be still. When we are in this new Practice of Stillness, that's when we can begin to focus on rewiring and releasing all the negative programming that has been dominating our lives for so long.

When we release, we transform. When we transform, we shift from a state of feeling constricted and contracted to a place of openness and freedom. Likely, most of us have not felt this way since childhood. Once again, feeling the exuberance of a child helps all of our senses and energies return to their best optimal place.

I do have to add this caveat: Undoing years of negative programming is not a "one-and-done" exercise. It takes a dedicated and consistent practice using all the tools I will be teaching throughout this book. It's a "show-up daily" and "practice makes permanent" way of self-healing our lives.

WHEN WE RELEASE AND TRANSFORM NEGATIVE PROGRAMMING AND OUR ENERGY IS OPEN:

- We go from smallness to a state of openness.

- We feel happy, positive, and loving.

- We feel creative.

- We feel connected.

- All functions of mind, body, heart, and spirit return to an optimal state.

Through Breath, Sound, Movement, and Meditation, you will give your internal operating system an upgrade. You can shift from contraction to openness, from stress and anxiety to resilience, from stagnation to *flow*.

STEP #3
CONNECT WITH LIFE SOURCE ENERGY

Source Energy is the source that gives us life—you, me, and every living thing on this planet. Some people call this God or The Universe, but by whatever name, it is the life force that flows through and connects everything. The uncertain state of our world right now is a direct reflection of a disconnect from Source Energy.

WHEN WE FEEL DISCONNECTED FROM LIFE SOURCE ENERGY, WE FEEL:

- Disconnected from nature.

- Unaware of energy or dismissing the idea of it as "too woo-woo."

- Disconnected from the source of your health, healing, happiness, and fulfillment.

- Separated, limited, and disempowered. We lack the confidence to make changes to our circumstances.

When we talk about connecting to Source Energy, oftentimes we try to make it philosophical and say dismissive things like, "I'm Christian, so I believe in God," or "I'm Hindu, so I pray to my Higher Power this way," and so on. But when we are talking about connecting with Life Source Energy, we take away the labels. This means you can practice this from any religion or spiritual/philosophical tradition. What we are talking about here is scientific and on the quantum level. We acknowledge that every facet of life is connected and communicating at all times.

That is the Life Source Energy I am referring to in this chapter.

THE 3 KEYS TO UNLOCK THIS WISDOM

All we have is now. The past doesn't matter because it is over and finished, and the future has not happened yet. All we have is the gift of this present moment.

So in this Moment of Now, we can work on the three things that will help us unlock a new Wisdom that will guide our self-healing journey. It's discovering an awareness and acceptance of what is really going on in our lives. Oftentimes, this involves facing really painful truths. Instead of avoiding this discomfort and emotional pain, we need to be able to breathe through it and begin to clear away the negative energy that no longer serves us with tools like breathing and meditation. We need to sit with this pain while showering ourselves with love, compassion, and patience without judgment.

I liken these moments of sitting in quiet observation to laying back and watching clouds go by. We don't try to control the clouds or even pretend they aren't there. We simply acknowledge and offer ourselves kindness and care during these moments of *awareness*, *transformation*, and *appreciation*.

AWARENESS AND ACCEPTANCE

When we come back home to our bodies, there is a period of time where we have to learn to feel safe and trust in our bodies. We need to cultivate and practice this feeling of safety to become **aware** of what is really happening and then **accept** those discoveries.

For example, one of the defense mechanisms our body activates when we are feeling unsafe is to move our eyes forward in our head. To move them back into place, we must achieve a feeling of safety. First, connect with your breath and heartbeat. I like to sit with one or both hands on my heart and just feel it beat. Then I come into awareness using my breath—nice slow inhales and long exhales. The key to getting our eyes back in place is to signal to the brain that all is well, and, to do this, you need to build awareness around you. I like to do this with my eyes shut but it works perfectly well with your eyes open. For example, if you are in your living room, feel the space in front of you and then push it out further, to the wall then beyond the wall. Expand further to the horizon and keep going. Now do this same sequence behind you, to the right, to your left, above you, and finally below you. When we bring awareness from all around us and expand it out, it lets the brain know that everything is safe in this moment and brings your nervous system to safety along with it.

Once we cultivate and practice this sense of safety, we can differentiate reality from the partial-truth stories that flood our minds daily. Our minds are meaning makers. Our minds and bodies just want to be safe, and so they create stories that serve us in the moment to keep us safe but, more often than not, have zero or at best partial reality to them.

Each part of us that has been injured has created a protector to make sure that we remain safe. Think how long you have been holding these stories inside of you, doing your very best to keep yourself safe. Part of healing is letting go of those protectors. As I release them, I always thank my protectors and tell them they have done a very good job. Part of acceptance is owning all of our energies, even the energy that no longer serves us. Sound therapy is one of the many ways to teach you to take that past energy and transform it into something more beneficial for yourself.

ACTIVATE, TRANSFORM, AND CREATE

When we activate and transform these energies that no longer serve us, we are putting our healing into action through our new practices, physical (breath and sound) and mental (observing and surrendering). When we go from a contracted state where our ruminating mind is constantly putting us into a state of upset to an open state of being where we have activated our own healing, we are now on the journey of **transformation**. Part of this journey is to use our imagination and visualize what we'd like to **co-create** with this healing energy source.

The best tool in our self-healing toolbelt for co-creating with Life Source Energy is Imagination. Modern society often links cultivating imagination with being unmotivated or "living with your head in the clouds." I disagree. Imagination keeps us in a state of awe, wonder, and growth. Feel free to stick your head in the clouds as often as you need to feel whole! The way we co-create with life source energy is by marrying our intentions in life with visualization. Through our visualizations, which is a form of guided and deep meditation, we leave our structured mind and come to a place where our identity no longer exists. As Dr. Joe Dispenza says, "We become nothing, no one, in no place, and no time. From this place outside the time-space container we co-create with life source energy using our intentions and visualized dreams for our future life. All of tomorrow is created in the Now."

GRATITUDE AND APPRECIATION

The act of gratitude is one of the most powerful ways to connect with source energy. When you are thankful for something, that usually means that it has already happened. Gratitude is when you are in a state of appreciation.

Deriving from the Latin word *gratus*, gratitude is defined as the quality of being thankful. It's an emotion that expresses appreciation; it is something we feel from a place deep within.

Medical studies have confirmed that an ongoing gratitude practice can have the long-lasting, noticeable effect of eliminating stress, deepening and slowing down the breath, as well as relaxing muscular tension.

I have a nearly daily gratitude practice that is one of the first things I do in the morning. It leaves me feeling centered, reflective, and ready to start the day from a place of fullness, abundance, and positivity.

HOW GRATITUDE AFFECTS THE BRAIN

In the last 20 years, a number of experiments have been conducted to investigate the power of gratitude and the impression it leaves on us. It turns out this lovely emotion is a catalyst to much personal transformation, with lasting positive effects on the brain.

In short, gratitude:

- Changes the molecular structure of the brain, literally rewiring it.

- Increases grey matter, which is associated with better cognitive functioning.

- Affects the limbic nervous system in ways that regulate our emotions, helping us to steer clear of toxic ones.

- Boosts the neurotransmitter serotonin and stimulates the brain stem to produce dopamine.

- Leads to enhanced activity in two primary regions of the brain: the anterior cingulate cortex (ACC) and the medial prefrontal cortex (mPFC) – the areas associated with empathy, decision-making, impulse control, and will power.

HOW GRATITUDE IMPROVES YOUR HEALTH

There's no shortage of positive effects gratitude has on the entire body, especially since the mind and body are connected. Here are some awesome benefits noted in studies observing the effect of gratitude on our health.

Being grateful:

- Makes us happy.

- Helps us release toxic emotions and manage stress.

- Lowers blood pressure and cortisol levels.

- Improves the quality of sleep.

- Motivates us to take better care of ourselves, such as by exercising and eating healthier meals.

- Strengthens our immune system.

GRATITUDE IS A NATURAL ANTIDEPRESSANT AND PAIN KILLER

When practiced daily, gratitude has the same effects as antidepressant medication. It is observed to boost serotonin and dopamine, the neurotransmitters responsible for happiness. This popular study by Emmons RA, McCullough ME. (2003) showed that participants felt happier and experienced less pain having recorded their blessings in a gratitude journal. Recounting the things we appreciate is what brings joy to our hearts and keeps us pain-free.

GRATITUDE HELPS WITH ANXIETY

Anxiety is an unsettling mental condition to experience, and these days there are so many people suffering from it. However, just a few moments of self-reflection on something that you are thankful for is enough to slice through those toxic thoughts. This is because gratitude activates the limbic nervous system in a way that regulates emotions and puts a damper on the ruminating chatter of the mind.

GRATITUDE HELPS MANAGE STRESS

A study by McCraty and Colleagues 2018 revealed an impressive 23% reduction of cortisol, the stress hormone, in participants who were asked to cultivate feelings of appreciation. 80% of those participants showed an increased coherence in heart rate variability patterns, which suggests they experienced a reduction of stress.

GRATITUDE STRENGTHENS THE IMMUNE SYSTEM

Studies show that pessimism and negative emotions weaken our immune system, while optimism and positive emotions strengthen it. Medical studies now confirm that our immune system flourishes, with higher numbers of blood cells, in response to positive emotions like gratitude.

GRATITUDE MAKES US RESILIENT TO LIFE'S UPS AND DOWNS

Cultivating gratitude boosts our resilience, both physiologically and psychologically. Our body learns how to bounce back easily after a stressful event. On a mental level, the positive mindset that gratitude builds helps prevent the downward spiral of worrisome thoughts. When we take the time to fully absorb ourselves in a quiet moment of appreciation, it feels like we have the power to bounce back from anything. We can take on any challenge that lies ahead of us.

GRATITUDE HELPS US SEE THE GOOD IN EVERY SITUATION

Wong and Brown's (2017) study revealed that gratitude begets more gratitude – It gets easier to arrive at a grateful state of mind the more you practice it. Each time we practice gratitude, we're rewiring our brains to see something positive in every situation, leading us to experience even more joy.

When you are appreciating something, like when you are outside enjoying nature, it means you are connected to Life Source Energy. Cultivate the attitude of gratitude daily.

YOUR BRAIN AND HEART

The way you are feeling and existing right now (in your unhealed state) is not the way you are meant to be.

Not now and not for the rest of your life. How many times have you tried to change a habit but just couldn't? How many times have you beaten yourself up for these failures? Have you ever disagreed with a parent, partner, sibling, or spouse, and there is never a resolution? And the very next time you disagree, you repeat the pattern nearly verbatim as the last time?

What if I told you this isn't your fault?

YOUR BRAIN

Many myths say that by the time we hit the age of 20, we start our downward decline in both brain and body function. It all depends on our genes. If you have good genes, you age gracefully and die at a ripe old age.

Recent DNA research completed by Dr. Bruce Lipton in the study of epigenetics says that isn't the case. How we think and feel has a significant impact on our bodies, brains, and lives. How we think and feel turns off and on various gene factors. Only 30% of our genes control our destiny. The other 70% is up to us.

Human beings are marvels of change, and we can create self-healing in our brains by thinking different thoughts than we usually think. Different thoughts create different emotions, which make other chemicals for our bodies to respond to than they're used to. By taking a conscious role in changing our brain function and using breath, movement, and meditation, we can become more vibrant than we ever imagined, no matter what age we are.

BRAIN BASICS

Let's think of ourselves as having three brains. Each area of the brain has a different function that takes us from thinking to doing to being. Let's explore these three parts of our brain.

1ST BRAIN: NEOCORTEX

The neocortex is our rational mind and the seat of our consciousness. This is also the brain sector where all our decision-making, reasoning, and rationalizing happens. It's the largest sector, making up 40% of the entire brain. Humans and dolphins share the most prominent frontal lobes among living beings on the planet, and this distinguishes us from other species. The Forebrain/Frontal Lobe is also known as the area of executive function. It's our CEO, our Creative Director, our Center. It has direct control over our free will, learning, creativity, and invention. It also controls our intention and our attention to the details and specifics of our lives.

It's the center that controls decision-making, how we behave, and also how we restrain emotional reactions. It controls how focused our concentration is. It also lets us speculate on outcomes and possibilities.

The first brain, our thinking and processing brain, allows us to learn new things and to have new experiences. Every time you learn something new, connections in the brain are made. Neuroscience research shows that an hour of focused concentration on one topic or idea doubles the number of links in the brain.

All of these new experiences and knowledge are stored in our thinking brains, the 1st brain. The entire brain is a map and divided up into its geography.

The back region of the neocortex is called the Occipital Lobe/Visual Cortex, and this is where our sight and spatial orientation are located. Our emotions live on the left and right side strips of the neocortex. The primary motor cortex also initiates and controls our motor function and movement abilities.

There are areas in the brain where our sense of self exists. Two areas of the brain that are important in retrieving self-knowledge, self-awareness, and perception are the medial prefrontal cortex and the medial posterior parietal cortex. Those areas are classified as our "non-self." It is what we deem "me" and "not me."

2ND BRAIN: THE LIMBIC BRAIN

Now, all this new knowledge and experience held in the neocortex won't do anyone any good if we don't process and apply them. The idea is, as we self-heal, we get our minds and bodies to work together.

When we learn new things, our mind activates all five of our senses and connects them to our environment. As the sensory information rushes back to our brains, thousands of jumbled neurons start to organize themselves into patterns.

As these sensory neurons begin to fire, the Limbic Brain activates and starts creating chemicals. The Limbic Brain is also referred to as the mammalian brain when our 2nd brain starts producing chemicals that make feelings, which become emotions.

As we bring new information and knowledge into the brain, the Limbic Brain creates unique experiences and emotions that begin firing our DNA and genes in new ways filled with new possibilities and outcomes. Our Limbic Brain instructs and shows the body how to respond to how our minds perceive and process things.

The Limbic Brain is also where the automatic functions of our bodies are housed. It's called the autonomic nervous system. It's the part of the brain that subconsciously regulates our heartbeats, our blood sugar levels, our hormone levels, respiration, and kidney function. This is the part of the brain that gives us our lives automatically without us thinking.

When our 2nd brain starts to make chemicals based on thoughts and experiences, it changes the body. Our brains and bodies are wise. If you've been able to create the experience once, you will be able to again. Just one time can create the same chemicals, thoughts, and experiences again and again.

Let me put this another way. If you think the same thoughts repeatedly, which create the same feelings and emotions in your body, you make permanent neuro pathways and connections in your brain. Things that fire together wire together.

When you have created an experience repeatedly, you have conditioned your body and mind to become one. When this happens enough times, your body knows how to do better than your mind, and it creates a subconscious pattern that you and your brain are chemically dependent upon. It becomes second nature, automatic. You don't even have to think about it.

This is what a habit is.

We've all heard the expression that we need to "break a habit." There are ways to accomplish this that give you the pilot seat and a spot to co-create your reality and self-healing.

When our Limbic Brain, our 2nd brain, has been activated repeatedly, it sets off and calls into play our 3rd brain, the Cerebellum.

3RD BRAIN: CEREBELLUM

The Cerebellum is the part of the brain that controls, and is responsible for, our memories. This includes both conscious/ implicit memories and those memories that we no longer consciously remember (called non-declarative memories). We've done things so many times that we don't even have to think about them consciously; they have just become who we are.

So, if we go from our thinking brains gathering knowledge to our 2nd brains where our bodies experience what we are learning to our 3rd brains which becomes our innate wisdom, then we go from thought to body to heart.

Years ago, I was a concert pianist and classical composer. The piano is an excellent example of the three brain functions. When I get a piece of music, I have to learn the notes by reading them and figuring out my fingering and where my hands are going. This is my 1st brain function, learning the music score.

The next step is to embody what I've learned: placing my hands on the piano keys and playing the music I'm reading while I create beautiful music. After learning the music score, I know I have embodied the music by physically playing the notes.

I have embodied the music by putting my hands to the keyboard and letting my ears hear the sounds.

I have embodied the music with the muscles in my hands and back that are physically engaging with the keyboard. At these moments, I am utilizing my 3rd brain function as I learn the score, fingerings, and dynamics by heart. I have played it so often that I no longer need the score; the music has become a part of my being.

THINKING THE SAME THOUGHTS EVERY DAY

Most of us think the same thoughts every single day. Did you know that 80% to 90% of our thoughts are the same as the day before?

Psychological research has shown that by the time we are 35 years old, most of our habits, beliefs, reactions to situations, perceptions, skills, and conditioned responses are subconsciously engrained and programmed within us. This means that we think the same thoughts every day, have the same feelings and reactions, believe the same philosophies, and hold deep convictions on these perspectives.

Each day we view our lives through the same lens, thoughts, and feelings as yesterday. By the time we are middle-aged, 95% of our thoughts and feelings, our programming, is running subconsciously. These have become automatic and are so deeply entrenched that not only is there nothing new happening, but we are also simply a memory of who we were the day before. We are a remembered being.

If 95% of our programming is subconscious, then it's fair to say that we only appear "awake." We are a living, breathing, unconscious version of ourselves.

So then is it fair to ask the question, if we think different thoughts, could they lead to new outcomes, behaviors, and possibilities? Could these new thoughts, which wire new neuron-circuitry, start to change the biology in our DNA, our genes?

The answer to these questions is YES. Research shows that when you change the way you think and feel, everything in your life changes around you.

With each different thought, your brain circuits connect corresponding patterns and sequences in various combinations that produce chemicals in the body equal to those thoughts. These chemicals are made to match your thoughts precisely to the way you were thinking.

This is on a loop.

As the body begins to feel the chemicals the brain is producing, it loops back to communicate with the brain how it's feeling in that moment, and the brain creates more chemicals to keep that feeling going. Your mind will create more thoughts that produce more chemicals and so on. We feel the way we think and then think the way we feel. This continual loop is called your "state of being."

COHERENCE

There is another issue we have to look at concerning the function of the brain, and that is coherence. Coherence is the order, rhythm, and synchronization where the brain functions exist. Coherence is a measure of the brain's ability to communicate through a clean, accurate channel between two sites such as the heart and brain. Coherence can also be measured by how effectively two sites are able to link and unlink as well as share information.

We live in an incredibly stressful and anxiety-producing world. Most people live under daily stress 70% of the time. When you're living in stress mode, your survival instincts kick in. This means that we perceive threats and danger in our external environment or personal living environment.

When we perceive that a situation could worsen, it deactivates our parasympathetic nervous system and fires up the primitive nervous system. We call this the flight or fight nervous system. When we sense danger, we will either flee the situation, fight to get the upper hand of the threat, or become small and try to be invisible.

When in stress mode, we will likely do one of these three actions. When a person is in stress mode, the only acceptable action to the mind and body is to try to control and predict the outcome of the situation.

When we are under stress, our body secretes stress hormones such as adrenaline and cortisol. This kicks the brain out of balance and has us looking from one thing to the next very rapidly. "I have to go to this meeting, and then go to this place, then complete this task by this time." Every time one of these rapid events fires, it sends a message to the neurological networks in our brains that there is an urgency and please send more stress hormones so we can make it through this day.

These hormones and rapid-fire attention-deficit make our brain fire out of order and incoherently. When the brain is out of order and incoherent, the rest of us is not functioning well either.

When our brains don't work properly, we don't work properly. It's that simple.

At this point, the brain is its own worst enemy and starts to attach itself to the conditions and circumstances of the person's thoughts and feelings. A healthy, stable brain fires as an entire entity. When the brain is incoherent, each section of the brain acts as a separate function, leaving the person with a brain that feels foggy, stressed, confused, and anxious.

When we live in our modern-day lives filled with stress, there are those three things the brain wants to do: run away, fight, or hide. In today's society, we're told that it's not acceptable to do any of these; we must face things head-on. Our brains are telling us to RUN, and society is putting the brakes on that idea. It's like starting and stopping at the same time.

When we're in this state, adrenaline is sent to the heart. The more stressed we become, the more our heart beats incoherently as well.

The moment your heart functions incoherently, you no longer trust yourself. The heart is one of the most intelligent organs in the human body. It thinks by sending signals to the brain. The heart contains neurons, the same type of neurons that exist in the brain, but the heart contains far fewer neurons than the brain, and their job isn't to think but to help the heart react to the various demands placed on it by the body. The neurons in the heart communicate with the brain by providing a feedback signal to the brain which affects our emotions. When we experience something physically, it changes our emotional state. When your heart goes to an incoherent state, it sends incoherent messages to the mind in a feedback loop. This is when the mind sends you into a state of imbalance and disease.

When we start to bring the brain and heart back into coherence and then create coherence between the heart and mind, this brings us back into health and balance. We also send more energy back to the brain, which gives us a different perspective and lens to look through. We become more aware because our brain and heart are coherent. It creates a greater space of consciousness.

When your brain and heart function coherently, your world begins to look quite different.

CHAPTER 3
YOUR BRAIN ON TRAUMA

BIG TRAUMA VS. SMALL TRAUMA

"One does not have to be a combat soldier or visit a refugee camp in Syria or the Congo to encounter trauma. Trauma happens to us, our friends, our families, and our neighbors. Research by the Centers for Disease Control and Prevention has shown that one in five Americans was sexually molested as a child; one in four was beaten by a parent to the point of a mark being left on their body. One in three couples engages in physical violence. A quarter of us grew up with alcoholic relatives, and one out of eight witnessed their mother being beaten or hit.[...]

It takes tremendous energy to keep functioning while carrying the memory of terror and the shame of utter weakness and vulnerability."

—BESSEL VAN DER KOLK M.D

In my studies, I followed Bessel Van Der Kolk, M.D. from The Body Keeps the Score Trauma results from experiencing or witnessing an incident or series of emotionally disturbing and/or life-threatening events. These events have a lasting and adverse effect on the person's ability to function on various levels, including mental, physical, social, emotional, and/or spiritual well-being.

From his work, I learned that there are two types of trauma.

BIG TRAUMA:

Psychology Today defines large "T" trauma as "an extraordinary and significant event that leaves the individual feeling powerless and possessing little control in their environment." Big Trauma can lead to feelings of great helplessness.

BIG TRAUMA INCLUDES:

- Natural disasters or other catastrophic events such as bombings or gun shootings
- Car or plane accidents
- Sexual or physical assault
- Combat or war

SMALL TRAUMA:

Small "t" traumas, according to *Psychology Today*, are "events that exceed our capacity to cope and cause a disruption in emotional function." These events aren't considered life-threatening but emotionally threatening as this type of trauma also causes people to feel helpless.

SMALL TRAUMAS INCLUDE:

- Conflict with family members
- Infidelity or divorce

- Conflict with a boss or colleague

- Relocating or moving

- Starting a new job

- Planning a wedding

- Having a baby or adopting a child

- Money and financial problems

Oftentimes, small "t" trauma is overlooked and perceived to be a normal event. Many people experiencing this type of trauma feel they are overreacting. These very thoughts are a type of coping mechanism called avoidance. We fail to process our trauma because we avoid acknowledging it as trauma and the impact it is having on us.

WAYS TRAUMA PRESENTS ITSELF

A trauma survivor develops a sense of coping skills to make themselves "feel safe." The greatest symptom of trauma is that the part of the brain that signals our fight or flight response is over-activated. Anything our brain perceives as a potential danger due to our trauma triggers the brain into a stress response. We could be triggered by something that is harmless in reality, like a text message or the smell of certain food, but because our brain has been traumatized, it perceives that event as a real threat and makes us behave as if we are at serious risk of harm. This can cause many issues when our behavior does not match our current environment.

HERE ARE SOME OF THE WAYS THAT TRAUMA PRESENTS ITSELF:

- Self-betrayal: Putting aside your wants, desires, and needs to be loved or chosen by another person

- People pleasing and accommodating: Fear of saying no because you might make someone angry. Avoiding people and situations because of the conflicts, guilt, or shame surrounded about wanting things for yourself or not wanting what they're wanting.

- Tolerating abuse and mistreatment

- Constant fear

- Needing validation and approval from others

- Lack of self-worth

- Disconnection and numbing: These are things like binge eating, eating disorders, unhealthy sexual relations, addictions, i.e., alcohol, drugs, shopping, distraction such as social media or talking on the phone constantly. Using a substance or an activity to avoid uncomfortable emotions and to regulate the nervous system.

- Dissociation and lack of engagement: When someone is physically there but mentally not present. They are mentally gone from their bodies and environment. This results in feeling like you're in a fog or haze and detached from what's going on. This can also result in losing memories.

- Codependency

- Overdoing

- Inability to be still

- Inability to receive

- Intense mood swings, ups and downs

- Denial

- Porous or extremely rigid boundaries

- Fixing others

- Manipulation

- Hyper-vigilance: The nervous system is in a fear-based survival mode. A person is hyper-aware of their surroundings and how other people perceive them. Such people are often diagnosed with an anxiety disorder when they are suffering from pre-frontal lobe trauma.

- Catastrophic perspectives: Viewing the world and the people in it as dangerous. It can appear like paranoia because these viewpoints lead to feeling like everyone is out to get you.

Every day people are responding and reacting to stress triggers. Most often, people feel this is just their personality: This is just the way life is. This is just the way they are.

But that's just not true. This isn't you. It's your trauma.

WHEN OUR BRAIN IS TRAUMATIZED, OUR MIND AND BODY LEARN 3 THINGS:

1. I am not safe.

2. I cannot trust. I cannot trust myself or those around me.

3. I must disconnect from myself to be loved and accepted by others.

All of these responses happen subconsciously. It's the brain's way of trying to protect itself from more pain.

One of the most important factors to starting the journey of healing trauma is to feel safe. One of the most important aspects of our mental and emotional health is that we can feel safe in our own bodies and around others.

When we can sit present with our trauma responses is when we can start healing them. It's important to know why we react the way we do. Many of these trauma responses and coping mechanisms were learned in childhood, when we saw the way our parents and adult figures in our lives responded to events and situations.

For the most part, we adopt these behavior patterns. These behavior patterns are deeply planted within our subconscious. Being a self-healing, conscious person requires having an awareness of our triggers and responses to those triggers, to discover who we really are and have responses to our trauma patterns that are in full alignment with who we are.

Your trauma is valid, and it deserves to be held and honored. Though we can't unring a bell, you can heal and transform from trauma. As we move forward in our self-healing journey, we will come to heal in the presence of our truth, compassion for that truth, and unrelenting love of oneself.

CHAPTER 4
HEARTFULNESS AND MINDFULNESS

Throughout this chapter, you will see me using the words *mindfulness* and *heartfulness* often. These two words are similar, yet also quite different. So much of our body's mental, emotional, spiritual, and physical health depends on our heart and its coherence within itself and with the brain.

WHAT IS HEARTFULNESS?

A Heartfulness practice is where we focus and connect with the wisdom of our heart and allow it to guide us along our journey. Heartfulness is a heart-centered way of life.

When we do Heartfulness meditation, we are focusing on the heart as a light, a blossoming flower, or an entrance to a cave or room to discover the wisdom that lives there, to restore calm to ourselves and our lives, and to access a doorway to our own higher intelligence.

In the previous chapters we went over what happens when our hearts and brains are not firing together in unison and the impact that has on our health and overall wellbeing. We also looked at what our fore-brain and our frontal lobe looks like after experiencing emotional and mental trauma. This can be a daunting reality but do not worry, I'm not going to leave you in this state.

Now that you have an awareness of how the brain and body function, there is a quick way to bring your heart and brain into coherence, alignment, and function. The HeartMath Institute in Monroe, Virginia, has been doing research on heart and brain function and especially around the topic of Heart Coherence.

Any time you are feeling stressed, overwhelmed, foggy, anxious, angry, frustrated, or irritated, try this exercise. Also, it works when you aren't experiencing negative emotions. It is always a good practice to do, so that you function at your optimal levels.

RAPID HEART COHERENCE TECHNIQUE

Step 1: Focus your attention in the area of your heart. If you feel comfortable, go ahead and place your hands over your heart and breathe in and out from your heart center. Breathe in for 5 counts and breathe out for 5 counts. Continue in this way.

Step 2: As you continue to breathe from your heart, in and out for 5 slow counts, activate a feeling of appreciation or gratitude you have for someone or something. Re-experience the feeling of love that you have for a person, a pet, a special place, or the moment you accomplished something fantastic.

This exercise creates a coherent state between your heart and head in about a minute. When we use our heart to create a coherent state between our brain and heart, we create balance between our thoughts and emotions, leaving us with more energy, more mental clarity, and the release of tension and anxiety.

When our brain and heart are in a coherent state, we have more balanced heart rhythms, our brain fires in a unified cohesive fashion, and we have more access to our innate heart wisdom and higher intelligence. We are then in a place to Thrive.

WHAT IS MINDFULNESS?

Mindfulness cultivates the present moment.

The clinical definition of Mindfulness is "paying attention to something, in a particular way, on purpose, in the present moment, non-judgementally." ~ Jon Kabat-Zinn.

Paying attention, in this sense, means paying attention to certain things you are surrounded with or in the present place and time. *On purpose* means you intentionally decide to pay attention to something specific. *In the present moment* means you focus on the here and now and get rid of any thoughts from the past or future. Being *non-judgemental* means you are not going to compare, judge or be critical of yourself or what arises while paying attention.

Some people believe that Mindfulness is completely about meditation and that can be a huge deterrent, especially if you are someone who has a hard time sitting still for any length of time.

More so, Mindfulness is about accepting all thoughts in the container and simply learning to observe them, learning how to incorporate meditation as a tool to assist you while practicing your Mindfulness.

Here are the topics and tools we will cover next to help you understand and enhance your Mindfulness Practice:

• Specific Mindfulness Actions

• Mindfulness Skills for Specific Mental Health Disorders

• Simple Questions, Thoughts, and Exercises

• Journaling Your Mindfulness Journey

It is my hope that cultivating Mindfulness skills will improve your mental, physical, and spiritual health and keep you grounded in the present. With regular practice, you will not find yourself letting your thoughts wander, and you won't get distracted by or caught up in the past or future negative thoughts. Mindfulness is a pillar in helping one live in the present moment, without judgement, and a step on the path of Thriving.

MINDFULNESS ACTIONS: WHERE DO I BEGIN?

Since Mindfulness is something that you can start at any time, it is just a matter of finding the time or making sure that you consciously think about incorporating it into your daily routine.

You have to remember that you are walking around with so many thoughts swirling around in your head at any given moment that you can feel as if you are unfocused, in a fog, overwhelmed, and your mind never has a chance to truly rest.

Mindfulness will help to declutter and clear your mind, calm your brain, and allow it to settle down for a spell. Have you ever picked up a snow globe and shook the snow until the entire globe becomes so filled that you can barely see the object inside? That is what is going on inside your mind in survival mode.

Once you start practicing Mindfulness, it will be as if the snow has settled at the bottom of the globe. You can see and think more clearly because you won't be straining to see through the hypothetical snowstorm of thoughts in your head. Instead of survival mode, you will be in Thriving mode.

To get you started practicing Mindfulness, use these simple exercises to get a jumpstart and overall feel for what Mindfulness is and how it can help you:

- Choose something to focus your attention on.

- Decide how you will focus: using your visual, auditory, or tactile senses.

- Focus "on purpose."

- How are you going to stay focused in the present moment?

- How does it feel not to be "judgmental?"

- Write what your definition of Mindfulness means to you.

FOCUSING YOUR ATTENTION:

By focusing your attention on a chosen mark, you are choosing a goal you wish to achieve by using Mindfulness. If you are on a walk, are you focusing on each step you take? If you are on a run, are you listening to each breath you take? In doing tasks such as these, you are hyper-focusing your attention on that task and that task alone. You don't let your mind wander but, instead, return your attention to the chosen mark or task over and over again, without judgment, every time your thoughts want to stray.

FOCUSING USING YOUR VISUAL, AUDITORY, OR TACTILE SENSES:

You can use Mindfulness in all areas of your life and wherever you are. We pass up so many beautiful moments by listening to all the noise inside our heads and not fully appreciating the beauty of any given moment.

First, decide what your intention is. Use your eyes to observe the color of the sky, water, buildings, etc., and notice every detail about them. Your eyes and attention are only on observing the detail and form of these things, not the noises behind you or the to-do list that keeps wanting to run through your mind.

Now, let us incorporate our ears and listen intently to trains in the distance or jets overhead. What do those sounds mean to you? Are they carrying passengers to a far-off destination with family and friends? Any sounds that appear during your Mindfulness Practice are totally valid.

Tactile senses are our sense of touch that is derived from a range of receptors in our skin. Now, let's focus on your skin. Are you making something with your hands? Are you feeling every brushstroke, every knit stitch, etc.? Are you petting your cat or dog? If so, your focus should be on paying attention to the softness or coarseness of fur and being present in this moment, having focused awareness, on purpose.

FOCUS "ON PURPOSE:"

As I mentioned previously, *on purpose* means you intentionally decide to pay attention to something specific. By focusing intently, you are making sure that you don't let your mind wander. That is why it is important to identify your intention before you begin. Notice what is happening in the moment and acknowledge it but let go of any distractions. Try to remain aware without changing anything. Observe and take in any and all observations.

When you become aware, you can eventually change unwanted patterns. It may feel extremely difficult now to focus without being distracted for even a couple of seconds, but trust me, it will come with practice and it will be worth it. You may not like the thought patterns you are observing now, but as you become aware of them and understand them, then you will be able to change them. You will be able to change them into thoughts that will heal you and help you to Thrive.

STAYING FOCUSED IN THE PRESENT MOMENT:

The world we live in is filled with distractions, so, you may be wondering, how are you going to stay focused in the present moment? We all have computers, tablets, cell phones, which are all meant to create or connect but which also fill our lives with noise and distractions.

Oftentimes, we are so distracted that we are not even aware of how much the "noise" has taken over our lives. When you practice Mindfulness, you learn to block out the noise and pay attention to your thoughts, your feelings, your physical body sensations, and your surroundings. At the beginning of creating your new Mindfulness Practice, it will be hard to let go of these distractions because they are so firmly woven into the fabric of your daily routine. But once you do, you will wonder why you did not set these mind-cluttering items aside for longer periods of time.

LETTING GO OF JUDGEMENT:

How does it feel not to be judgmental? That might be a hard question at first because, for many, being "judgey" is a hardwired habit. But we need to re-wire this habit into something that serves us better. Without distractions and with the new healthier habit of focusing on one thing, you notice everything about the present moment and the object of your intention. This is the state where you become non-judgemental.

Your current thought patterns might consist largely of criticisms you're thinking about yourself or others and false conclusions you've drawn about various situations. When you observe the present moment, your mind is not cluttered with criticisms and false conclusions, and you will find yourself open to feeling sensations that you might not have felt in a while. You are not being distracted by other thoughts, feelings, or physical limitations.

Let's pause a moment to sit with the teachings I just shared. If you are able, grab and pen and paper (or a keyboard) and write what your definition of Mindfulness means to you. After you spend time in Mindfulness, write down what happened. What did you notice?

If this sounds intimidating, know that you don't have to start practicing Mindfulness for an hour a day. Start out slow, maybe 5 minutes. You can gradually build up your Mindfulness practice a little at a time. After all, this is your journey.

THE BASICS OF MINDFULNESS

When you begin practicing Mindfulness, you are not doing a total "brain dump" but directing yourself to focus your attention on a chosen target. By focusing on a target, you can bring yourself back into focus whenever your mind wanders.

No one is perfect, and with all the thoughts that our brain produces each day, it is normal to have moments where you can't help but have your mind leave the present.

The goal is to keep your focus and only notice the distractions and your emotions as they creep their way into your Mindfulness session. Make note of any stray thoughts or emotions that arose during your session. Were there any physical sensations you might have felt?

Because there is no way to completely shut down other thoughts processing in your head, your mind will wander from time to time. If you do find this happening, take a moment to stop your Mindfulness and make a note of the thought, but then let it go and move on. After you release the thought, return your mind to your chosen mark.

The intent of practicing Mindfulness is to fine-tune your ability to become more and more focused, overcome mental obstacles, explore your feelings, and help you to take the time to look within yourself.

What if you already have a Mindfulness Practice in place? Sometimes, it's beneficial to revisit the basics just to keep our Practice sharp and clear. Ask yourself these questions:

- Are you taking the time necessary to practice intently? Mindfulness takes daily practice.

- Are you finding excuses not to carve out a few moments of time in your day? What can you do to change that? Everyone can come up with excuses, but it is the person who genuinely wants to benefit from Mindfulness who will find the time.

- Are there old habits creeping back into your Mindfulness sessions (check your phone, being distracted by housework, etc.)?

OBSERVING YOUR MINDFULNESS PRACTICE

Journaling your experience will allow you to look back and see how far you have come. It's fun to look back at our initial objections to see how silly they really were.

When journaling about your Mindfulness Practice, ask yourself these questions:

- Was I able to relax?

- What did I do to stay focused?

- What smells, sounds, colors, memories, thoughts, feelings, mental pictures, or body sensations did I discover?

- What are the feelings I had?

- Where did the emotion start in my body?

- Was I able to distinguish the present versus the past or future?

- Did I focus on my emotions as an observer? What was the story behind the feeling?

- Did my thoughts have a theme to them?

- Did you engage in an inner dialogue to allow yourself the ability to erase the thought?

Talk about how you know it is normal to have these thoughts and that you are not going to allow them any control and you are not going to engage with them while you are practicing Mindfulness.

THOUGHTS

As mentioned earlier, we all have thousands upon thousands of thoughts that enter our mind each day. It's not about trying to get your mind to stop thinking; it is what you do with those thoughts after you notice one creeping in. In order to dismiss the distracting thought, you need to observe it, accept it, and then let it go by choosing not to deal with it at the present time.

If you were sitting at home and watching a TV show that didn't particularly interest you, you would change the channel, right?

The same principle works for your thoughts as well. You can deliberately choose what you want and do not want to think about. If you are sad, angry, or worried, you can change the channel, so you don't have to watch or participate with what is going on.

Whatever you are thinking about is what affects your feelings and behavior. We can choose to ignore bad thoughts and only think about thoughts that make us feel good or better.

There are times when you just can't help it, and the negative thoughts become consuming. What you choose to do with them in that moment will say a lot about your emotions. If someone has anxiety, depression, or ADHD, they are focusing on and internalizing negative thoughts which originate from false core beliefs and fears. These internalized negative thoughts will play over and over like a scratch on a record unless something is done to "move the needle."

These negative thoughts become our feelings, and the more we feel, the more we think the same thoughts. When our feelings become the means of our thinking, it becomes almost impossible to change. It's so much more than "just think positive thoughts." This is about changing how you think, act, and feel to create a new personal reality.

Every day, we think about 70,000 thoughts. 90% of them are the same thoughts we thought the day before. To enact and embrace change, you have to become aware of your unconscious thoughts and behaviors and modify them. You also have to look at those emotions which keep you anchored in the past and decide if those emotions are coming with you into the future.

One of my big hurdles to get over was the grief I felt for my siblings' deaths. They died many years ago in a car accident. I was 19 years old and lost three of my siblings. To say it traumatized me is an understatement. My grief and trauma from that enormous loss ran the operating system of my life and body for decades. In my healing, I had to look at my thoughts around this and the stories I told myself, such as, "I'm the last one standing" and "I'm all alone." And let's not forget the horrible sadness that I just couldn't get past. All the times my girlfriends would get together with their sisters or siblings brought to the forefront the great emptiness I felt. So how to get past this? The facts are the facts. My siblings died in a car accident nearly 40 years ago now, but my body and mind remembered that moment as if it was happening in the present.

To heal this part of myself, I noticed what repeating thoughts I had about this situation and how frequently they came up. I wrote them all down in my journal. This made it come alive and be a concrete thing as opposed to wandering around in my mind. Then, using Mindfulness, I simply observed when these thoughts and feelings came up, not judging the feelings and thoughts but just accepting them as being there. In time, I reflected both in my journal and with my therapist about if these emotions are continuing to serve me. After much dialogue and introspection, I came to the conclusion that, not only had this grief become my identity and personality, but it had also held me prisoner. I chose to create a new personal reality that served me and their memory in a better way. My sadness has greatly decreased, and my ruminating thoughts and the identity I anchored to myself about the event have gone. My new personal reality is that a terrible event happened in my family and that I am resilient and have moved forward, thankful that we got to be siblings. To make this leap and change after so many years, I had to become greater than my feelings and my memorized self.

I share this with you because I know that asking you to "change the channel" or "move the needle" will not be simple, easy, or quick. What we're talking about is nothing short of changing the entire landscape of your mind and how you experience life, the world, and yourself. It may be daunting, and many of you might be thinking that it's impossible—but it's not. You can change the thoughts that shape your reality. By becoming the observer, noticing your thoughts instead of being carried away by them, you can begin to see yourself and your reality differently, in a way that best serves you to help you live your best life.

PART 2
CREATING
NEW WAYS
OF BEING

CHAPTER 5
SAFETY, TRUST, ACCEPTANCE, AND SURRENDER

Healing is coming to a Place of Safety, Trust, Acceptance, and Surrender. You cannot heal unless you feel safe and trust your body. You cannot heal until you accept where you are. You need to acknowledge, embrace, and welcome surrender to clear the old energy so new, and healthier, gifts can come into your life.

One of the most powerful techniques in healing your mind is your body. Let's begin.

SAFETY

Our bodies are meant to be a safe home for our spirit, but this can be very difficult to relearn for someone who has experienced trauma.

For people who have been physically or sexually abused, their bodies can feel dangerous and even become a source of shame. Asking someone who has been through trauma to love and feel safe in their bodies again might, at first, feel wrong. Just know that now is the time to believe that safety within us is possible.

To shift our mindsets and patterns to healing, the ability to feel safe is so important. We need to rediscover, relearn, and allow ourselves to accept the feeling of being safe in our bodies again. Yes, I know. You may be thinking, "Easier said than done!"

I understand. I've been there.

The first steps in healing have to do with feeling safe within our own bodies, but most of us are so disconnected from our bodies that we focus on things OUTSIDE of ourselves (money, jobs, relations) to feel a sense of security. We need to come home to ourselves. We need to learn what it feels like to be safe in our bodies again. To live a self-healed life, we need to actively rediscover that heartfelt sense of home, peace, and comfort in our skin.

Sit with that for a moment, and let it settle in. We have to reprogram all of that conditioning that tells us we are not safe out of our bodies.

I have spent decades living in the programming of my mind on avoiding pain and not feeling because I didn't feel safe inside my own body. Women, in general, have spent decades living inside their own programming that it's not safe to feel and it's not safe to feel inside our bodies.

I know I am asking a lot here. You may be thinking, "What if I can't handle all of the emotions coming up? What if I feel unsafe with my loneliness, sadness, or grief when I dig deep into this new knowledge?" At this moment, if you need to spend some time reflecting on this or even doing some journaling, I highly recommend it. These moments of reflection may be needed before you can move forward.

Despite what your conditioning and programming is telling you, the truth is that your body is the safest place to be. It's time to come home to yourself.

The idea of 'coming home' might be very complicated for you, as your trauma may have originated in the home. But I can assure you that this homecoming is not one filled with fear and hidden agendas. It is one where you are embracing and appreciating your body and your life wholeheartedly because you have made the decision to love every part of yourself again.

No fear. No hidden agendas. No "survival mode."

Just love, acceptance, and safety.

Regardless of external circumstances and relationships, connecting with the wisdom of the body will give you that sense of wholeness that you long for.

It's OK to be vulnerable and do the work you need to create a practice of self-healing. Just know that you can handle anything. Our bodies are our own best medicine and healers. Your body will not give you anything that you can't handle.

When we are young, and our safety is compromised, we develop coping strategies, which oftentimes comes in the form of avoidance. We don't have to process or deal with issues or discomfort that we actively avoid. At least, that's our rationale at the time. In reality, we are creating ways to **avoid being in our bodies**. Examples of what avoidance looks like include staying busy all the time and hyper-scheduling every moment of our lives, so we don't have a moment to stop, feel, and simply be.

Choosing avoidance can also take the form of what I refer to as numbing strategies, using food, alcohol, drugs, relationships, sex, shopping, or scrolling on social media. We choose to "numb out" because we are too afraid of feeling and feeling uncomfortable. And it's not your fault. This is the mind's natural response to trauma when you are not ready/able/safe to fully process what has happened. It's a form of self-protection that has helped you survive, but now you are in a place where you can heal and thrive.

Never judge yourself for your coping patterns. That might sound difficult because we are so good at being mean to ourselves.

The biggest mean girl around is our own personal "Inner Bitch," who is always running a reel of self-doubt, self-judgment, and deprecating comments in the back of our minds. This is the time your Inner Mean Girl needs to sit down and be quiet because her influence on your life is coming to an end.

Instead of sitting in judgment of your own actions and thoughts, I encourage you to **question why** you behave this way. I promise that's when the door opens so that you can reflectively see things in new ways. This self-reflection shouldn't be approached as if it's meant to be a punishment. Be curious in your questioning. Be interested in why you react this way. Ask yourself. "Why is this my pattern?" or "When did that start?"

Become curious about your triggers. Acknowledge why it hurts or is uncomfortable when you pursue exploring where they came from.

It's when we acknowledge our patterns that we can shift them and have awareness around them. If we don't, you know what happens. They play out again and again and again and again.

We have all of these triggers, and on top of that, we create coping mechanisms to deal with these triggers. Each time we cope with a trigger, instead of healing it, our world becomes hypothetically smaller, and we slip into the habit of living a limited life. I hear from so many women that they feel like they've disappeared. We turn inward and hide our life goals because explorations and dreams feel terrifyingly uncertain.

In a sense, we're afraid of feeling.

If this sounds familiar, it's time to open that up and understand your triggers, which is an important part of your self-healing journey. Understanding our triggers allows us to do the healing as they arise, to move through the anger and the pain, disrupt our old patterns, and replace them with new ones, so these past triggers and wounds no longer have control over our lives.

Maybe once upon a time something really bothered you, and you gathered some awareness around it and did a little healing around it, and now that something no longer bothers you. You had gained insight, healing, and a complete shift in perception. That's transformation, and that's healing.

True transformation happens at the intersection of pain and love.

When we are triggered and feel pain, rather than disconnecting from it, we can go into our bodies and love that pain with all we have. You might be thinking, "How do I love my pain?" or "That's impossible. I hate my pain. My pain is ruining my life so why on Earth would I want to love it?"

"Through Love all that is bitter will be sweet, Through Love all that is copper will be gold, Through Love all dregs will become wine, Through Love all pain will turn to medicine."

— RUMI

You were raised to believe that pain is something you need to run away from, something you should avoid at all costs, because it may make you look weak. But I'm here to share that pain, just like all the good, positive, and blissful emotions that you are so fond of, needs to be felt. Your pain demands to be felt.

In the moments in your life when pain comes knocking at your door, it will want your undivided attention and focus. When that happens, I invite you to welcome it as you would welcome a life-long friend. Because pain is there to point out the things in your life that are out of balance. If you learn to work with it instead of working against it, it will help you carve through the rough walls that have been imprisoning the real you for all these years. It will help free you from a world of fear and lack.

Pain did not arrive on your doorstep and in your life with the intention to hurt you. Greet it as a teacher as it frees you from all those fearful thoughts, ideas, attachments, beliefs, and limitations that keep you unaligned with your true self and Source.

Love the pain, and let it show you the way to heal. That's what creates transformation at the deepest level.

We live in a wildly wonderful world, but also a world that is inundated with self-deprecating messages directed at women. "She was asking for it," "That's woman's work," "A real lady wouldn't act that way," or my least favorite, "A man can do it better." We are constantly bombarded with messages that tell us we are never, ever, enough.

I am here to assure you that you are in fact more than enough. You are perfectly made, and you deserve only the very best in life. You are the hero of your own story.

TRUST

You cannot take a self-journey unless you are dealing with the issue of trust. Boundaries that create trust are a must.

Every one of us is already trustworthy, and we deserve to trust ourselves. Why? Because we already have what it takes to be reliable. In addition to the individual talents and skills each of us brings to the table, we all possess the natural wisdom inbuilt to the human form—***intuition***.

Those who choose to compare themselves to others often perceive the other person to be "more capable." As if we already know that they know they have everything they need to live a thriving life.

In reality, no one really knows what is going on behind the scenes in that assumed "perfect life." All of us are struggling with unseen worries and issues and fighting battles that no one else can see. So, put away your hypothetical measuring tape, because you are on an equal playing field with everyone else in the world.

What is going to be available to you when you're fully trusting yourself? Even if you haven't made this connection to trusting yourself yet, you can start by simply saying, "I'm excited to trust myself one day."

In doing this, we begin to trust ourselves again. In doing this, we unlock our inner power of knowing. We can tap into that place that always knows.

We just need to choose to listen.

ACCESSING TRUST IN OUR BODY

Once we start to settle in and feel our emotions and become the observer of our feelings, we can trust the experience.

There are two ways to deal with our emotions: as either the observer or the identifier.

OBSERVE OR IDENTIFY

When we identify with our emotions, we think that we are our emotions.

I **am** sad. I **am** anxious. I **am** depressed.

Versus

I'm **feeling** sad. I'm **feeling** anxious. I'm **experiencing** depression.

We are all the result of energy. Thanks to this energy, we are constantly moving, shifting, and changing. As human beings, we are always in motion. Energy in motion equals **emotion**. Energy in motion *is* emotion.

When we acknowledge that energy is directly connected to emotion, we also tend to think that we *are* those emotions. But that's just not the case. It's easy to slide into a habit of saying "*I **am** depressed*" instead of separating our physical self and reframing it as the more accurate, "*I am **feeling** depressed.*" Our feelings are not labels for who we are as people. So why do we think this way?

Because we are all constantly evolving, we unconsciously put pressure on ourselves. If we're sad, that state of existing suddenly feels very, very BIG. So, we say, "*I'm such a sad person.*" Or if we're anxious, "*I am an anxious person.*" We unknowingly assign this state of being like it's our new permanent destiny in life.

Not so.

These observations are emotions, and as I mentioned above, energy in motion **is** emotion. Being able to "call ourselves out" when we fall into the pattern of "*I am such a __*" instead of "*right now, I am feeling___*" is a thought pattern that needs to be rewired for us to begin to access trust in our body.

I was someone who identified very closely with the emotions of sadness and depression. I know now that I was in a deep state of grief for the life I thought I was supposed to be living. I would attach sadness and depression to my identity and carry it around like an anchor. This hypothetical anchor of describing myself as "sad and depressed" affected every facet of my life. I thought this was just the way life was, and I was a product of my life situation.

In reality, this just wasn't the case. I know now that I was experiencing moments of despair. I know now that I was experiencing periods of depression. But I, my self, and my being **were not those things**. I had taken up residence in the space or essence that sadness and depression exist in.

But it was not a permanent address.

Slowly, I learned to change my relationships with my sensations, and to do that, I reminded myself that I was an **observer**. I was the one watching and paying attention to those heavy emotions of sadness, depression, or anxiousness. I was not part of the definition of those feelings. I was not embedded into those feelings. Instead, I was the non-judgemental narrator of my life that honored the essence of who I was as a creator, teacher, musician, mom, CEO, and woman.

This new viewpoint gave me distance from my feelings. It allowed me to step back and drop the burden of viewing my constant state of upheaval as the total of **me**. Because of that, I gained new clarity and began cultivating healthier thought patterns that would ultimately lead to trusting myself. And with that self-trust, my intuition rose and became a huge part of my self-healing.

And it is my wish that this will happen for you as well.

So, let's talk about intuition. What is intuition? Intuition seems to defy logic or any normal process of reasoning or previous knowledge. You usually have feelings of intuition at a moment's notice. Intuitions come to us in all forms: feelings, warnings of danger, a dream.

When it comes to intuition, we all have it, and women seem to be especially tuned into what we often call our "gut feelings." Unfortunately, our intuition often ends up taking a backseat when our minds are cluttered with fear, uncertainty, sadness, and despair. The moment we begin to unearth (and listen to) our intuition is when we can start to *trust* our intuition. Our natural-born intuition will speak up and be heard instead of being drowned out.

I'm sure many of you are thinking, *"I don't have intuition"* or *"I'm not an intuitive person."*

I can assure you that you **do** have it, and you **are** an intuitive person. Intuition is the deep and wise intelligence of the body, and it is something that has been with you since birth. It's the place in our bodies where we both expand and contract. It's the place where our visceral and authentic, **Yes, No**, and **Maybe** live.

We are all very familiar with the **NO** feeling. Think of a time when you knew deep in your gut that something wasn't a good idea. Pay attention to that **NO** feeling; our intuition is rarely wrong.

What about those moments when everything feels **so good**? You feel full of energy and inspiration. The things that you are doing, experiencing, and achieving just feel **right**. That's your internal **YES**. These are guiding factors on our path of the discovery of life, and we all are lucky enough to get to tap into it and follow it if we choose.

So why don't we pay more attention to our intuition? What tends to happen is, when we get those intuitive hits, the mind takes over and begins to question. Like I mentioned previously, our brain is always trying to figure things out. Suppose we allow the brain to start running its preprogrammed audio reel of *"yeah, but…"* or *"what if…"* We fall into the trap of overthinking. This inner conflict drowns out what we should already know: to trust our intuition, we need to trust ourselves.

If you truly want to practice Mindfulness and incorporate it into your daily routine, you have to be willing to become "in tune" to your intuitions and inner wisdom. You already experience being in tune when you get the butterflies in your stomach or the "gut" instincts you feel from time to time. We will call this our Mindful Intuition Practice.

Mindful Intuition means practicing meditations that help you connect with your inner wisdom and/or intuition. Relax your body before you begin your Mindfulness session.

Completely focus on every inch of your body while at the same time relaxing each part. Start at your head and go all the way to your toes.

After you relax each part, allow yourself to be taken on a journey. Where are you going? Where do you want to allow yourself to be taken? Relax. Focus on whatever is taking place in this calm, quiet place.

Stop and observe a moment of silence. Think about your Mindful Intuition. Has intuition been a large part of your life?

Have you always followed your instincts/intuition? What are some times when you wish you had or hadn't allowed your intuition to take over?

How do your intuitions come to you? Thoughts? Dreams? Journal about anything you can remember that has to do with this session.

When we let the intuition itself have a voice, we can start living an intuitively driven life versus a life based on reason, logic, second-guessing, overthinking and allowing our mind to ruminate like a runaway train. Before I began my self-healing journey, I was always trying to think my way out of my life's problems and issues. Because of this, I was in a constant state of mental turmoil and physical exhaustion. I used my brain to stay in a state of control (or so I thought) instead of recognizing my emotions for what they were and using that to fuel my life.

After decades of trying to achieve that false sense of control, I can vouch that it doesn't work.

Then, I came to a place of surrender, and it all changed. When arriving at this new place of surrender, my mind quieted, my intuition sharpened, my body came to a place of Center and Alignment, and the healing work began.

As you go through your day(s), I'd like for you to become aware of these sensations in your body. Especially that intuitive **NO** that lives in your gut. Become aware of when your neck and shoulders feel tight. When your lower back hurts so much, it hurts to move. When headaches become a regular and disruptive part of your day. When your skin begins to experience breakouts or the tic in your eyelid never seems to go away.

All of these things are your body talking to you. These are your emotions showing up in and on your body.

I'd then like you to become aware of what a visceral **YES** feeling is on your body. Think about decisions you've made in the past where you just *knew* you were on the right path and making the best choices for yourself. Ask yourself which of those moments gave you tremendous joy and happiness. What did that feel like in your body? What did it feel like for you when those happy moments and decisions happened for you?

The final visceral emotion I'd like you to become aware of is your definite **MAYBE**. Your intuitive MAYBE pops up when uncertainty is front-n-center. MAYBE is the middle ground when we are not feeling a confident YES or a passionate NO. What does uncertainty feel like in your body? What moments or situations cause your intuitive MAYBE to arrive? Are you at a solid MAYBE because you need more information? Because the idea, act, or experience is 100% new?

If you're unsure how to come up with these answers, start asking yourself questions that are a definite "no," such as, "Do

I live in Antarctica?" Most of us have to answer NO to this question. What does that feel like? Ask yourself if you are called something different, such as, "Is my name David? Is my name Alice?" State a name that isn't yours. Ask yourself a favorite food question for either yes or no answers. Are my children named X, Y, and Z? Use their real and fake names to evoke clear feelings of *Yes* and *No* in your body.

Think of a time when someone asked you to do something, and you weren't sure if that's what you needed to be doing. How did that feel? Ask yourself a question about going out to eat at a new restaurant. You could go either way. How does that feel in your body? What about getting together with girlfriends, even though you have to work the next day? How does that feel in your body?

Your body will give you the intelligence you need to answer these questions. With this exercise, we build our awareness and intuition about how our body reacts to the emotions, thoughts, and feelings going on in our lives.

As with physical exercise, these questions work to refine the muscle of our intuition. The goal is to hone our "intuition muscle" to use it, follow it, and trust it. The wonderful thing is that when we use one of our practices, such as breath, our access to our core body wisdom is so much greater. We feel our way into trusting ourselves and our bodies.

ACCEPTANCE

We tell ourselves inner stories that keep us trapped. These stories are filling us with stress and anger that feed our chronic illnesses or mental distress. These narratives can sometimes make us feel like our lives have been stolen. That was the case for me. After almost six decades of "trying to survive" narcissistic scenarios, I felt like I was living a life wasted. And I felt intensely angry about that.

Stress, anger, and worries are bullies, and we are the only ones who suffer when we give them space in our minds and bodies. When we let these stories of stress, anger, worry, and guilt gain power over us, we are basically surrendering our mental well-being to these "bullies." We are, in a sense, giving them permission to stifle, limit, trap, and frustrate us. And, as you know, when you feel all of these negative emotions, it's very hard to believe in dreams, healing, and the possibilities of who we are and who we are meant to be.

But just know that your past does not define your future. During your self-healing journey, you will be "flipping the switch" that quiets the mental bullies and lets you see clearly how you are worthy of all the love and abundance in the world.

Accepting that truth is the foundation of all that you will learn in the coming pages and beyond. We need to accept that we weave together stories in our minds that work to keep us small, hurting, and feeling undervalued.

It's time to let yourself out of your own mental cell and choose freedom.

When we think about making a major lifestyle change, such as starting a diet and exercise regime, deciding to stop smoking, or saving money, what ends up happening is that our minds draw from its vast database of evidence of why *this isn't going to work.* We are going through the motions physically, but our minds are thinking, "Who are you kidding?" As you can imagine, we are doomed even before we can begin, and it's no surprise that these ambitious plans fail.

The result is once again feeling like we've let ourselves down. It's so easy to turn this into new layers of self-doubt and negative self-talk. "I knew this wasn't going to work. I'm just not trustworthy. I don't have the willpower to do things. I can never do this."

Sound familiar? We all have a lifetime of self-deprecating stories that we have told ourselves and continue to say to ourselves.

Our role and devotion in this self-healing journey are to re-structure those stories that nag at us in our heads, to literally *re-story* ourselves into a place of center and authentic alignment with who we are, a place of knowing with every fiber of our being that we have strength, value, and purpose. This is where Acceptance begins.

So, what is your new story? We are constantly evolving, constantly changing, and continually growing. We are continuously moving forward, and our lives and stories are changing with us. As of today, fill your heart with the knowledge that the past that no longer serves you is now a distant memory. The past only equals the future if you decide to live there. The past will no longer define your future, and together we will choose to embrace the present moment that we're living in. Today, we get to choose what stories we're going to create, and we do that in this very present moment. It's time to shed old, dead layers like an onion and emerge renewed. When we consciously choose to co-create what happens in our lives and what happens in our bodies, a shift occurs. Over time, thanks to these Moments of Now, we will create well-being, health, abundance, and happiness in our bodies and lives.

In our journey of trusting, accepting, and surrendering to the wisdom of our bodies, **we are coming home**. We can't heal something if we hate it, if we're afraid of being in our bodies. We can't move forward in self-healing if we are uncomfortable in the skin we are in.

It's time to change the toxic relationship with our bodies to one of loving admiration.

When moments happen when you are spun back into feeling uncomfortable or untrusting of your body (and they will happen), pause and put some distance between what you feel and what you truly are. Remind yourself to observe the uncomfortable feeling in your body, then shift to a place of being neutral with it. Just know, this momentary discomfort and doubt will pass because you are learning to feel safe in your body and trust your intuitions as well. When we choose a state of neutrality, it's much easier to change to a **place of love** as well as **acceptance**.

And when we come into a place of acceptance, that is what a self-healing journey is all about.

Creating a life of self-healing, safety, trust, and acceptance is not a "one and done" activity. Like any other discipline, "practice makes permanent." We need to show up daily to be able to stay focused and "re-story" ourselves. The stories that we tell ourselves, especially the old, familiar patterns from our past, are always ready to slip back in when we least expect it.

When I first realized this critical truth, I felt anger. The anger came from the realization that I had let people tell me who I was, and wasn't, for far too long. And the knowledge that I gave those opinions power over my life left me feeling furious. At them, but especially at myself. Sometimes, just facing the reality that we are oftentimes our own worst prison guards is a bitter hypothetical pill to swallow. But, once I was done being mad, I also realized that I was the only one who was allowing myself to stay in that state of darkness. My old stories (the disabling and destructive ones) were a prison that I had locked myself in because, in a twisted and sad way, they were familiar.

It was time to let myself out of my cell.

The stories we tell ourselves have unbelievable influence over our actions, habits, and decision-making. We need to make the stories that we tell ourselves loving ones that come from a place of forgiveness and acceptance.

Immediately.

Our self-healing depends on it.

SURRENDER

What does it mean to be in a state of surrender? What does it mean to be in a place of allowance?

When I am struggling with something in my life, whether that be a personal health issue, business, or family matters, I always have to ask myself, "What am I resisting?"

Suffering and struggle come when we are resisting the flow of what needs to unfold.

When we resist something that appears in our lives, we subconsciously think, "It's uncomfortable, so I'm going to take charge and resist it. The way to stop feeling poorly is to control it, change it, and manipulate it." As long as we are trying to force something different from what's present, we're not honoring life's cycles and what truly needs to unfold.

What we know to be true is that everything is happening for us in perfect timing. Say this, "Everything is happening for me in perfect timing."

Now, I live my life by this knowing, this inner wisdom. I don't believe things happen by coincidence or by accident. There is no such thing. Everything is happening for me in perfect timing.

When things happen to us in life, instead of labeling things in polarities such as good/bad, right/wrong, we need to realize it's just what it is. This is just the way it is for the time being. Just like seasonal storms dissipate, these times of unrest will as well. If something feels uncomfortable or is full of drama and difficulty, this is a time to shift perception and ask, "What's the lesson in this?"

If I'm suffering or struggling, I get to come back to that place of inner knowing and ask myself with curiosity, observation, and non-judgment, "What am I resisting right now?"

When you get in an argument with a loved one or a disagreement at work, do you catch yourself trying to manipulate the situation, so it appears to be the other person's fault? Maybe you unconsciously do this without realizing it, just to feel the relief of pressure from yourself. Sometimes it can be the other person's fault, but oftentimes it's not about fault or blame at all; we project our hidden feelings and operating system onto the other person, playing out our inner conflicts externally.

These are the moments when you need to tap the brakes and ask yourself some hard questions about the urge to deflect blame onto someone else.

Do you feel that there is an emotion or spiritual wound inside you that needs to be healed? Did you need to discover something about another person? Did you need to learn something about yourself?

Now I'm going to say something that will be difficult for some of you to hear.

Everything shows up in our lives *for* us.

Even when it looks terrible, challenging, or complicated, it's happening *for* us.

Not *to* us.

So, sit with that a moment if you need. Then ask, "What are the hidden lessons in all of this?"

The teachable moment here is that it's easy to be present in the moment when life is joyful and happy, but, when the wind of life gets stronger, more challenging, demanding, and complex, that's the time when we all need to lean into the wind instead of seeking shelter from it.

Like a windmill, we can use those moments to stand up straight in a high wind. We choose to stand up to the gusts that threaten to topple us over and ride the gale instead of being blown away by it.

So, when those harsh winds of life blast us in the face, we can choose to bend like a reed and navigate it with strength and determination. Remember, it's the stiff and unbending trees that are the first to be snapped off in a storm.

But while you are riding out your life storm, please pay attention and acknowledge that there is a divine reason each situation is happening. The answers to the "why" will reveal themselves when you allow and surrender to this new awareness.

When we are in constant resistance, we can't discover what's wanting to be uncovered and unearthed. The thing that triggers us is our body's way of alerting us to what needs to be self-healed.

What we resist persists. If we don't allow these things to come up, the pattern will repeatedly continue in many different circumstances until, finally, we surrender and look at what needs to be self-healed.

These insights often start in our physical bodies. We have an intuition about something, and we don't listen. The next time the message gets a bit louder and comes up emotionally in our bodies as anxiety, depression, frustration, or stress. If we continue to resist it, it shows up physically in our bodies through physical ailments.

Physical manifestations are emotions we haven't paid attention to or acknowledged.

Can you ask yourself, "What am I resisting?" After you've answered that question, is it possible to let go?

Again, this comes back to trust. Can you trust that the wisdom of your body can shift and communicate things in a different way? We can't control anything, but we can create our experience and influence. We can influence our focus, influence our energies, and influence visions of what we want.

When we surrender to what we've been trying to resist, we allow the magic to come in. When we hold onto the things from our past so tightly and keep running them through our minds constantly, we do not have space for the magic and wisdom to drop into our lives.

Suppose you're holding onto a relationship or job for dear life because you've convinced yourself there may not be anything better. Guess what? There is no room or space for the universe to work its magic and drop something better in.

You don't get to experience that love and joy and fulfillment from a loving relationship because all your energy is holding on to a toxic one.

You don't get to experience the success of being valued and respected or progressing in your career because you are holding on to the unfulfilling job you're in, as if there is no other choice available. When you just let go, the universe can work its magic.

When we let go, we let in the traits and truths that are in true alignment with us and our highest values and potential. Instead of being attached to something that weighs us down mentally, emotionally, and spiritually, we free ourselves from the things that no longer serve us.

So, the allowing part of this equation is to allow ease, joy, happiness into our lives. To heartfully allow good health and abundance into our lives. To welcome and allow well-being into our lives. Introduce your body to the idea of flow. In our breath and movement practices, you will embody the practice of energy flow and then watch it appear in your life. How awesome does it feel to be in the flow of life energy instead of constantly resisting it?

We have become so addicted to the way we think life and things should be that we control it and fight for it to make it happen a certain way. We're all trying to achieve something here. Just let that urge go, surrender, and see what walks into its place.

Yes, this is hard, but through breath and movement, it shifts.

Let it go and let it unfold, because the gifts that life has for you are so much greater than what you're currently allowing yourself to receive.

CHAPTER 6
COMING INTO PRACTICE

Whatever has brought you to this place in your life, you are here because you are ready to transform your emotions and your experience of life.

The next step is what I like to call "Coming into Practice."

Coming into Practice is the process of rediscovering who we are at a core level. Unearthing this part of us will bring us into a deeper connection with other people.

Practice is the opening of the heart so that we can feel joy and happiness, as well as sadness and sorrow, without shutting down. It is the opening of the mind to have the awareness that includes everything and excludes nothing. It is the recognition that *we are all the same.*

Practice includes clear observation, acute and active listening, and allowing ourselves to respond to the moment with compassion, as opposed to reacting out of conditioning.

This mindset shift is a commitment to regular and ongoing practice, not a one-and-done solution. It is a going forward, a change in lifestyle that nurtures mind, body, and emotions. It is a Practice that will be woven into your daily life that offers the gifts of improved health, enhanced wellness, and enhanced mind-body function.

The Pillars that I will be covering in the following pages are ones that I've embraced and studied over decades. They do not pretend to be easy, simple, or quick.

These ancient practices consider the great complexity of the human being and through heartfelt and sincere practice, through embracing the skill of each practice, we will become peaceful, happy, and free from our mind and our pain.

It doesn't matter what has happened to you in the past or where you find yourself in the present, the most important thing is your intention to break self-limiting beliefs and self-paralyzing thoughts and behaviors to find your freedom through Practice.

In order to create this new way of being, we need to begin **right here**. We need to begin Practice right **where we are right now**.

WHAT IS PRACTICE?

When we practice, we deliberately create time so we can slow down to find a natural rhythm to support our well-being. Putting more space, emotional space, in our Practice allows us to reflect and respond instead of reacting to the situations in our life.

Are you ready to begin your self-healing journey? Before you begin, there are things we need to be clear on.

PRACTICE IS DIFFERENT FROM EXERCISE

The number one thing that we all have in common is the fact that our mind constantly ruminates. We are the sum of our circumstances, and we spend a shocking amount of time worrying, churning, strategizing, and having hypothetical conversations with people who aren't listening to us.

But when we know better, we do better, and in Practice, we can unhook the ever-ruminating mind. We can instead welcome a Practice that includes meditation, breath, movement, and sound that calms the mind and brings us to stillness.

With this comes a way of creating new wiring and firing of the neurological synapses in our brains so that our mind **not** ruminating becomes the new norm. This doesn't mean it will be totally silent "up there" or that we will be in a state of apathy; it means we will no longer be in a state of panic or anxious reacting. You come to a place of Centered Observation, and you will proactively decide what you are going to interact with. It's like you've turned the slo-mo camera on, and you have time to mindfully, and thoughtfully, respond to a triggering moment.

YOU BECOME THE OBSERVER, NOT THE REACTOR.

When we accept where we are, as ugly as that may be, we can realize that we have all the choices. This applies to how we react to others as well. As our mind begins to heal, we become capable of *not reacting* to the demands of the people in our lives, particularly the ones who know how to trigger us. A healing mind and heart are able to respond with "I hear the urgency in your request, but I need to take a moment to think about that."

You no longer have to react the way your abuser or your disease wants you to.

This is healing.

If stress and anger are a consuming part of your thoughts, I want to encourage you to use mindfulness exercises to lower your stress response. Allowing your body to stay at high-stress levels can be extremely dangerous in certain situations depending on your physical makeup. Making a choice to use some of the exercises outlined in this section, you can reduce your stress considerably just by remembering to practice the following habits:

Body Scan: Control your breathing while paying attention to every part of your body, from the crown of your head to your toes, and noticing how it feels. At the same time you are noticing each part, concentrate on releasing any tension your body is holding onto.

Relaxation Breathing: Take deep breaths in to induce relaxation and peace and allow your exhales to be long as you let go of tension and worry. At the same time, notice each part of your body and concentrate on releasing anything that needs to be released.

Muscle Relaxation: Tense every muscle in your body slowly and methodically. Then, release the tension by starting with your head and ending with your toes.

Remembered Wellness: Again, start with the breathing techniques as outlined above, but for this technique, remember a time when things were good in your life.

Journaling: Journaling your experience will help immensely so you can capture each moment and then have a record to look back and see how you were feeling, what you were thinking, and/or what worked and what didn't work.

THE JOURNEY OF HEALING AND AWAKENING

The journey of healing and awakening using the practices of breath, movement, meditation, and sound is not about gathering new information or techniques. It is about deepening your capacity to embody and integrate these practices and activate their transformative potential in your own mind, body, heart, and spirit.

We are coming from a closed and contracted place, one that holds pain, injury, dis-ease, trauma, and brokenness, to a place of openness. The tools of the practices, whether used alone or together, will help us access our place of happiness, health, and well-being.

Every single one of us who comes into Practice is carrying around emotions and feelings of woundedness. No matter how hard we try, we cannot get past it by thinking about it, talking our way through it, or saying daily affirmations. The skill that is greatly needed at this point, when all other attempts have failed, is how to *listen*. We must develop the skills of deep listening so that we can resolve and move through our own deeper issues.

For many of us, our deepest issues reside in our implicit memories, the ones we cannot consciously recall but are stored in our unconscious mind and in our bodies. By now, we accept that we cannot rationalize our way out of our pain and trauma. We need to access the wisdom held by our implicit memories.

Many of us have tried to heal from our wounds by working through our conscious memories, but the truth is that our conscious memories are highly unreliable. Research has shown that our memories are distorted, manipulated, and sometimes completely made up.

Think about a family event, such as a wedding, a funeral, or a birthday party. It is an amazing thing to hear how each person who attended the event witnessed or experienced something completely different than the person they were sitting next to. Our bodies, however, are completely different. Our bodies remember everything. Our bodies do not interpret, rationalize, or assess; they simply hold an energetic imprint of the memory or, in this case, the trauma. The body keeps the score.

We have to remember that when we are experiencing a trauma trigger or "hot spot," it is because one of two things is happening. The first is your body is either responding to something in the present moment which is upsetting, or it is responding to a trigger in the present moment which is setting off a triggered association, a memory from your past which is creating the feelings as if the traumatic event were happening now.

We do not need to explore every dark corner of our minds or dredge up every past experience to have a powerful change. I want to be clear here: you don't need to 'recover' your implicit memories. For some people, this could be extremely harmful, and I would never advise anyone to attempt this without the proper supervision of a professional. What I am suggesting is for you to pay attention to your body's response to triggers so you can use the Four Pillars of Self-Healing—breathwork, meditation, movement, and sound—to shift them.

Your body, right here, right now, holds everything you need to heal and let go of those trauma imprints on your mind and body.

INDIVIDUALITY

When we come into Practice, we are approaching the modality, whether that be movement, breath, meditation, sound, or all four, as an alignment between the wisdom and voice of the body.

When we are in the early stages of crafting a practice, it begins as a mind-centered practice. Am I moving correctly? Is my breath correct? Which sound do I make? Which sound will do the best job of healing me? It is all cerebral and analytical. As we are being very efficient and disciplined, we are not listening to the body.

However, when we shift and begin to add deep and active listening to the many ways in which our bodies speak to us, when we embrace both the way our body feels as we are now holding trauma and the bodily feeling of unfolding and discovering our original self, we stop worrying about the particulars or feeling that something is wrong with us, and we start trusting and tuning into the body's wisdom.

We make choices that are correct for *ourselves* and what our bodies are needing, instead of being in our head and trying out the latest fad, method, diet, etc. All of those things exist outside of us. Inside of us is where the jewels lie, the gold nuggets to our healing.

FROM THE BODY UP

Several years back my daughter, Zaina, gave me a profoundly personal birthday gift. She wanted me to feel what it was like to be in my body. From her perspective, I had completely disconnected from my body. At the time, I could not understand her meaning of "being disconnected from my body." I had no context or vocabulary to process that. She set up an amazing week of sessions with yoga practitioners who helped me connect my breath with my body. They helped stop my mental chatter and had me sense where my feelings were placed in my body.

Throughout the week, I went to a variety of therapies, ending my body birthday week with a group sound meditation under the big blue whale with 800 people at the Museum of Natural History in New York City. It was a truly incredible experience. Thank you, Zaina!

Her gift showed me that, to resolve our trauma, we have to develop a very deep and personal relationship with our bodies.

Now, that doesn't mean that those who already do mind-body-spirit connection practices are necessarily connected to their bodies. Within your own yoga, qigong, Pilates, tai chi, or dance movement practices, you might be primarily focusing on how to do the postures correctly, how the flow and patterns of the movements connect together, and where the correct breath pattern fits in. Are my biceps rotating outward enough in downward dog? Is my back foot at the right angle in Warrior One? Exhale chaturanga, inhale up dog. Oh my goodness, when will this chair pose be over?! Sound familiar? These are all part of learning, but they're still the technicalities.

Oftentimes in the mind-body healing modalities, we are encouraged to override feelings and practice non-attachment. We are also used to taking instructions or, if we are teaching these modalities, giving instructions. Many of our physical practices, our breath and sound practices, our meditation practices are still being run through our mental filters.

But what if, instead of those other questions, we asked ourselves, "Where am I feeling these movements in my body?"

As we create our practice, we start with the body and work up towards the mind. We cannot think our way through this. As we learn the movements and patterns of yoga, qigong, dance, tai chi, or Pilates, we learn the movements by heart so that we can bring them into our practice at home, away from class, and work with them slowly to sense and feel the emotions our bodies are processing as we practice the movements. As you practice more circuits, repetitions, and flows outside of class, your body will become more integrated with your daily life.

WHEN WE FEEL, WE HEAL.

Once we feel, we can move the trauma out of our bodies. When we feel, we begin to process, unwind, and better understand our own bodies. As you move, breathe, and listen, it is ok to find yourself crying, laughing, feeling joyful, shaking, or simply finding new perspectives from an unexpected "new" position.

Part of coming into practice is to realize what already exists in your body without manipulating it. Your body tells its own story. By learning where and how your body holds its trauma, you come to understand that story, and that is how you heal. Healing begins when we become friends with our bodies. So often we think, "When I reach this hallmark or place, then I can love my body, love myself." But actually, loving ourselves is the first step. We have to be our own best friends.

When we befriend ourselves, we have someone to dialogue with. If we remain separated or disconnected from our bodies, we have no one to negotiate with and remain in our trauma states and hot spots.

Practice is not a temporary situation. It's showing up daily, no matter what, and doing what we can. It takes immense patience, self-compassion, and focus. We can get to the point where our bodies no longer hold us back but release us into a life of freedom.

When we feel different in our bodies, the world outside of us looks different too.

CHAPTER 7
THE FOUR PILLARS OF SELF-HEALING: BREATH, SOUND, MOVEMENT, AND MEDITATION

The Four Pillars of Self-Healing could be written about in volumes of words if we were to dissect each one individually and delve into them fully. My goal with this section of *Thrive* is to bring awareness and to touch on just the basics of Breath, Sound, Movement, and Meditation.

As you move forward with creating your own Self-Healing Practice, some of these Pillars (or all!) may pique your interest and make you wish to seek deeper understanding. I highly encourage your own research and self-discovery! This is how you learn, experiment, and grow. Even now, I am still learning and honing my own version of the Four Pillars of Self-Healing. If you are looking to pursue deeper learning and understanding, my advice to you is to do your homework and research your particular issue. Between your local public library and the internet, at your fingertips, you can delve much further into each subject.

When you are in touch with your mind and body, and know how to effectively use Breath, Sound, Movement, and Meditation, you will find yourself living in a much more peaceful state!

BREATH

Disclaimer — Breathwork is NOT advised if you have a known cardiac arrhythmia (including very slow heart rate), a history of heart block, or are taking certain antipsychotic medications.

Our breath is expanding and contracting. Think about this; every breath ever taken is still in the air. When I breathe, I breathe the breath of my ancestors, and everyone else's ancestors too.

The one thing I know you and I have in common is the act of breathing. The very fact that you're reading this right now means we're both living, breathing beings. That's a really good thing.

Breathing is the only system in our bodies that is automatic and is happening right now without us needing to think or act. Breath is also under our complete control. Learning how to breathe and paying attention to your breathing are important skills to have when creating a self-healing journey. When you change your breathing patterns, you change your physiology.

Just by breathing in and out, you are triggering parts of your nervous system that you probably weren't even aware of. Some parts that are involved are your heart rate, your sweat glands, your digestive system, and your intestine and glands.

Breath is a powerful tool that we can use to connect to ourselves. Breathwork allows us to look through healing with a different lens. A lens which is ours and ours alone. No more needing to live through someone else's lens and expectations. Breathwork brings us into our own space to view ourselves authentically. Breath connects us back into our intuition and true essence.

In order to allow yourself to feel more calm and less anxious, you need to practice breathing techniques which will lower your stress response and improve your emotional and cognitive health. Why? Because, at any given time, we have three areas in our bodies that are communicating. We have the chatter in our minds of thoughts and judgements. We have our emotions. Then underneath that we have our intuition. In our culture today, we identify most of the time with our thoughts and our mind. Our emotions are part of the feedback loop that feeds the mind in its constant ruminating state. With both emotions and thoughts running the programming, we find ourselves unnecessarily in the fight, flight, or freeze mode because our body and mind think we are under attack.

That 'under attack' sensation can happen in the most unexpected moments and situations. Have you ever been washing the dishes, driving the car, packing your suitcase, or trying to go to sleep when all of a sudden you start thinking about someone or something in your life that causes you anxiety or stress? You might be completely oblivious of the effect your thoughts are having on you. In these moments breathwork can help you become aware of and be free from the feedback loops that keep you in fight, flight, or freeze mode.

Our mind-body system is designed to move into a stress response, fight or flight, for short periods of time to deal with dangers when they arise and then to release tension, shake off the anxiety, and restore relaxation in the body.

When your nervous system becomes caught in fight or flight mode (sympathetic nervous system activation) long past the time of the perceived danger or stress, the doorway to your intuition and spiritual connection becomes bogged down and clogged with an overload of information. Like a receptor or antennae receiving too many signals all at once, you are unable to hear, feel, or sense your inner knowing and intuitive connection.

During a time of crisis, we can intuit a sense of knowing and right action. This "knowing," or intuition of right action, is well known to arise in emergency situations, however our system is not designed to remain in this heightened state for long periods of time.

Our breath is the connection between our body and mind. The breath is what shifts us from our heightened brain state and back into our bodies. The breath is also the link between our conscious and subconscious mind.

Many people try to **think** their way into feeling better, but unless they tap into their body's natural abilities, trying to force comfort and calm will only cause even more stress!

In breathwork, we release the mind and emotions and tap into our intuition, our inner knowing. In that state of expansiveness, there's no forcing things to happen. There's no resistance. It just is. It is exactly by tuning into the natural flow of our breath that we learn how much better and centered we can live by surrendering to the wisdom of our bodies. Our bodies know how to keep themselves alive and what they need to thrive. If we learn to trust our bodies, we can align our lives with the natural flow of universal energies, discover wholeness, and find peace.

The breath brings us to the perfect spacious moment of now.

Breathwork lets you release chaos and everyone else's beliefs and come back to what is true for you—come back home to *you*.

There is a reciprocal, two-way street happening when we do breathwork. For each emotional, physical, and psychological state we find ourselves in, we have a related breath pattern that goes with that.

FOR EXAMPLE:

The way we breathe when we are calm is different from the way we breathe when we are angry or upset.

When you change your breathing pattern, you can also change your emotional, physical, and psychological state. It's all within your control. We can use the breath to get into our nervous system, as well as our immune system, and choose the state we want to be in.

When we control our breath, we choose self-awareness, we choose self-control, but more importantly, we choose to be connected to our own healing energies and be free from our emotional, physical, and psychological pain.

HOW DOES BREATHWORK WORK?

So you may be thinking, how does breathwork bring us to that deep sense of peace, contentment, and healing?

ACTIVATING THE PARASYMPATHETIC NERVOUS SYSTEM

Your frontal lobe is home to your parasympathetic nervous system which is responsible for the body's rest and digestion response when the body is relaxed, resting, or feeding. It basically undoes the work of sympathetic division after a stressful situation. Our parasympathetic nervous system is the opposite of our sympathetic nervous system, the wiring in our brain that is connected to our fight, flight, or freeze mode.

When we tap into the parasympathetic nervous system and mindfully make our exhales longer than our inhales, our brains and bodies are able to shift to "rest and digest mode."

While breathing in specific patterns, your blood becomes hyper-oxygenated, allowing you to exhale much more CO_2 than normal. When we do that, we go into a state called respiratory alkalosis, which means our blood becomes more alkaline. This creates a unique situation of having a lot of oxygen in your blood ready to be used, but because of the lack of CO_2, it can't be absorbed easily by your cells or your brain. When our blood becomes more alkaline, we shift our perceptions and perspectives. Your body temporarily slows down the prefrontal cortex of the brain. This is the part of the brain that holds emotions, makes decisions, judges yourself, and overthinks.

So as this part of the brain slows down, it suppresses the pre-frontal lobe functions, leaving your body and emotions free to feel and process at a much deeper level. When we stop the breath pattern and come back to normal breathing or a breath hold, the CO_2 starts to build back up and sends a huge rush of oxygen to the brain and the cells in your body.

STIMULATING THE VAGUS NERVE

Another benefit of breathwork is that it deeply stimulates your vagus nerve. The vagus nerve represents the main component of the parasympathetic nervous system, which oversees a vast array of crucial bodily functions, including control of mood, immune response, digestion, and heart rate.

As we do breathwork, it increases our heart rate variability, sending a message to our nervous system that we are safe and that your nervous system should switch into rest and recovery mode. This leaves us feeling really good and connects us even deeper with our heart and our emotions. The heart and mind become synchronized and come into coherence. When our heart and mind are in sync, you are not operating from fear or overwhelm or reactivity but from a place of alignment.

LOWERING CORTISOL

When we include breathwork in our self-healing practice, the body responds by lowering the stress hormone called cortisol. Cortisol, the primary stress hormone, increases sugars (glucose) in the bloodstream, enhances your brain's use of glucose, and increases the availability of substances that repair tissues. Cortisol also curbs functions that would be nonessential or detrimental in a fight-or-flight situation. As we're doing breathwork, you can feel immediately, after just a few patterned breaths, that you are, in a sense, calming your cortisol/stress responses. Mindful breathing will help your body naturally shift from an anxious state, a fear-based state, into a very calm state.

ACTIVATING THE LIMBIC SYSTEM

Another incredible thing that breathwork does is activate the limbic system. The limbic system exists in the amygdala section of your brain. The amygdala is nearly in the very central interior of your brain. When we are stressed or in fight, flight, or freeze mode, the amygdala actually increases in size. As we begin to breathe and hyper-oxygenate our blood, the amygdala gets smaller. It is a well-known side effect of breathwork that memories and emotions will come back to you. The amygdala controls the emotions and memory sections of our brains, and as we help it through breathwork, memories and emotions get recalled.

When stressed, we forget things, like to lock the house or to send that email or to get milk at the store. Practicing breathwork regularly can bring us more clarity and presence. If you've ever tried to remember a dream, it's sort of like that.

Also, a symptom of trauma is that you can't remember your childhood or have only a few memories. You might even be missing some adult memories as well. This is our brain's way of protecting us. Through your breathwork practice, as you begin to feel safe and trust your body, memories may float up to the surface of your mind. Because you are in a relaxed state, you are simply observing the memories as they come forward. You are not attached to them, nor do you identify with them. For myself, long lost memories seem to surface days later when I'm out for a walk or brushing my teeth. Being triggered can happen, but I invite you to just observe what has come up for you, not attaching to it or making it part of your identity. Simply observe. All emotions, memories, reactions, and feelings are welcome in a breathwork session. As we breathe for even a couple of minutes, your brain unhooks and your body feels safe and these amazing and good feelings take over the body. You live completely in the moment, feeling really good.

5 BENEFITS OF BREATHWORK

1. IMPROVES IMMUNITY & REDUCES INFLAMMATION

A fast-breathing pattern stimulates the immune system and decreases our inflammatory response. In today's world, most people have unconsciously developed chronic inflammation, which is the starting point for many diseases such as heart disease, stroke, cancer, diabetes, chronic kidney disease, arthritis, bowel diseases and non-alcoholic fatty liver. Lowering our inflammation is hugely beneficial for overall health.

2. BUILDS RESILIENCE

As we drop our cortisol levels through our breathwork, it creates strength and resilience in different body systems such as the immune, respiratory, and cardiovascular systems. Each time you do breathwork, it's like lifting weights and training your muscles. You get stronger each time you do a session.

3. MAKES YOU HAPPY

No kidding, right? We're all happy to be breathing, but more than that, science is proving that doing breathwork can affect pleasure neurotransmitters like dopamine and serotonin. People who practice breathwork report having greatly improved moods.

The first time I did a breathwork session with activated breathing patterns, I went in without any expectations. I had the most incredible experience. I felt extreme joy and happiness in every cell of my body, and I continue to feel it in my ongoing practice.

4. HELPS IN REVERSING CHRONIC ILLNESSES

I have seen many witnesses and testimonials of people who have reversed their chronic illnesses, such as multiple sclerosis, fibromyalgia, rheumatoid arthritis, Lyme disease and other autoimmune related paralysis, type 2 diabetes, depression, and anxiety. I have suffered from both depression and psoriatic arthritis, and I can attest that breathing has been a major catalyst in my healing.

5. IMPROVES ATTENTION AND MENTAL HEALTH

When we breathe from our diaphragm, also known as diaphragmatic breathing, it improves our attention and reduces stress levels. In 2017, the NIH did significant studies that show diaphragmatic breathing significantly decrease negative self-talk and self-image.

TETANY

Now let's talk about cramps. No, not that kind...the kind that might happen during a breathwork session. When we do activated breathing patterns, energy builds up in our bodies and ends up settling in the hands, feet, lips, and other places in the body. We can feel cramping and stiffening in our hands, feet, lips or even the back of our necks and so on. Let me say here that it isn't dangerous. When we breathe in breathwork patterns, tetany, for some, is the way the body responds to letting out CO_2 and bringing in lots more oxygen.

The actual tetany is happening everywhere in the body, but one is going to feel it in their hands and extremities. The energy is building up contractions to get ready to release.

Tetany can be a bit uncomfortable, however there is a quick and easy solution to release the body when tetany sets in. Tetany is always manageable. If you experience tetany and a part of your body, like your hands or feet, is actually cramping and hurting, release the breath pattern and go back to normal breathing until your hands or feet relax. When you are ready, you can return back to the breath pattern.

I'm a breather that doesn't suffer from tetany, or so I thought. One day, about a year into my practice, I was doing a breathwork session, and for the first time ever my hands went numb and my lips were tingly. I was taught that whenever this happens, we have the physical effects of tetany but there is also the spiritual/emotional reason for having tetany.

Tetany is an invitation to ask ourselves, "What do I need to let go of?" Then I visualized myself releasing and letting go as I exhaled. My hands and lips relaxed and went back to normal. Making sure our exhales are longer than our inhales is how we release tetany in the body.

WHAT DOES BREATHWORK "LOOK" LIKE?

By simply breathing in your nose and out your mouth you are mindfully working to calm your physiology and stress responses. This mindful breathing shouldn't only occur during mediation or sound therapy. Mindful breathing, breathing in through your nose and out through your mouth, can be done throughout the course of your day. You can do this mindfully before you answer the phone, before you eat something, or if you are feeling stressed.

You can also do diaphragm breathing which involves taking in so much air into the lungs that it expands the stomach. When you practice a chest breath it is simulating anxious breathing. When you take in air and allow it to fill your diaphragm it is considered relaxation breathing and provides more oxygen to the body to help lower the stress response.

In order to breathe through your diaphragm properly, place a hand above your belly button and one hand on your chest. Next relax your abdomen and breathe in through your nose and fill your lungs allowing them to expand downward. Do not breathe shallow breaths and do not raise your shoulders. Exhale slowly through your slightly opened mouth. You will know if you are doing this correctly by the warmth or the coldness of the breath. If you are breathing from your abdomen, the air will feel warmer whereas if you are breathing from your chest, the air will feel colder.

Paying attention to your breathing in great detail will help you practice the process of noticing when your mind begins to wander and can help bring your mind/attention back.

If you journal about your breathing, keep track of what happened. What thoughts or feelings surfaced? Did you notice if your mind started wandering? What did you like or dislike about paying attention to your breathing? What other thoughts did you have?

When you show up to do a breathwork session, you are taking actions, proactive steps, to care for yourself, to express emotion, heal, relax, and reconnect, even to move beyond your mind and body to come to a spiritual place. As you connect with yourself, you create the ability to connect with others. As you heal, your community and the world itself heals.

As author Mark Nepo says, "When we heal ourselves, we heal the world. For as the body is only as healthy as its individual cells, the world is only as healthy as its individual souls."

Before healing can come to our children, our families, our friends, communities, and ultimately to the planet itself, we must first show up for ourselves every single day and do the great job of healing ourselves first. We cannot bring healing to another until we have healed ourselves.

SOUND

Aside from the heart, hearing is the first thing to develop in utero, and it is the last thing to go when we transition out of this life. Sound can only be experienced in the present moment.

We use sound in the form of music, as it has both negative and positive impacts on our lives and is a large part of celebrations, grief, worship, and other various ways we communicate and process. For thousands of years, many cultures have relied heavily on sound and music to carry forward beliefs, celebrations, and final passages.

At a very young age, I recognized that songs were used to create connections with people. For centuries, "song keepers" were community members in different cultures who were tasked with being the "keepers" of traditional songs. These Song Keepers were also in charge of keeping the songs, celebrations, and rituals alive within the community. They were tasked with passing that wisdom onto the younger generation. Alongside each elder song keeper is a young person standing alongside to learn the songs and the dances and rituals that go with them. The younger generation then, in turn, can continue to keep these traditions alive and train the next generation.

In the Baltic area of North Karelia, Sapmi, and Gotland (where my family is from), song is so important. We are known as The Song Lands. We use song, voice, and heart in our common practice of family song rituals. These Song Rituals are an important part of life. Milestones like birth, the naming of a new baby, coming of age, graduation, marriage, and passing through the veil are all steppingstones into the well-being of the family and the community at large. They are also a part of healing processes like taking a sauna. During these important milestones, the Song Rituals are at the core and are usually sung by an elder woman in the family with several younger women, young women, and girls participating as Song Keepers in training.

When I lived in the Middle East for years, I noticed that chant, song, and recitation as well were always at the core of healing, comfort, and celebrations.

I have been blessed throughout my life to know experience the profound effect and healing powers of sound, and I am excited to share that knowledge with you.

MY BEGINNINGS IN MUSIC

I came from a very musical family. My family used to love telling stories about me demanding to sit in my sister's lap as she played piano, and by the time I was three, I was requesting that I be able to take piano lessons too! Sound and music were very much a part of my childhood, and the love of both followed me into adulthood.

From there, I immersed myself in becoming a concert pianist and also earning several degrees in music. I paired my love of piano with my love of teaching and was a certified music teacher for many years. As a teacher, I worked with children, teens, and young adults, not only teaching them how to play but also the art of music theory and composition .

My love of music and sound continues to guide my path in life to this very day.

In the 1990s, I had the privilege of taking several masterclass workshops with a brilliant music therapist named Don Campbell. Don was an authority, and a believer, in the use of music as a way to heal, and he also authored the book *The Mozart Effect*. His teachings deeply resonated with me.

I eventually left my role as a teacher to raise three wonderful children and share my love of sound and music with them as they grew. Over the many years of my music study and appreciation, I accumulated a prolific collection of all genres of music. I began creating what some would call "mixtapes" of the different types of music that made my heart sing. Then CDs came along, and I found I had a knack for creating compilations of lovely and calming music CDs that my surgeon husband would give to his patients to listen to before surgery. These compilations were very much appreciated in our community, so I began creating music compilation CDs for patients who were navigating the post-surgery process to bolster their healing. It was never anything I did for compensation; I was more than happy to create these CDs as a way of being of service. It was during the years of my creation of these CDs that I witnessed the impact that music had on the body's healing process and a patient's state of being.

During this time, I also became familiar with an oncologist named Dr. Mitchell Gaynor. He was well-known as a respected and knowledgeable physician, but also as one who moved outside of the mainstream comfort zone. According to an article in the ASCO Post, his fascination with using music as a tool of healing began when he cared for a refugee Tibetan monk named Odsal, who had a very rare cardiac condition. A practitioner of meditation, he schooled the monk in his own style of meditation, and they quickly became friends. The monk reciprocated by bringing a traditional Tibetan metal singing bowl to Dr. Gaynor's Manhattan apartment.

Dr. Gaynor was deeply aware of the way his patients suffered through cancer-related surgeries, chemotherapy, and radiation and noted that the process of recovering and healing from a cancer diagnosis was a deep and painful one. Determined to lessen the discomfort and encourage the body to heal, Dr. Gaynor began playing Himalayan singing bowls for his patients who were doing cancer treatments to give them reprieve and find deep rest from their treatments.

After noting the significant and positive results, Dr. Gaynor did comparative research on patients who were using sound therapy against those who were not. He determined that using sound therapy in conjunction with traditional cancer treatments elevated the body's ability to heal itself. Those who did not include music therapy in their treatment process showed a decrease in remission and overall healing. During his research and studies, Dr. Gaynor confirmed that vibration touches every part of the body and that everything in our known universe is sound. Every person, place, animal, and plant has a vibrational existence.

Even material and unseen immaterial things have a vibration. Our entire universe, world, community, home, job, etc. are layers upon layers of vibrations. Some vibrations are resonant and others dissonant. There are silent parts, complex rhythms, and singular melodies. All of these elements create our heard and unheard, but *always felt*, soundscape.

Fast forward many years, my adult daughter became very interested in the practice of yoga as a way to relieve her own stress and anxiety. She became so in love with this modality, she dove deeply into the study and practice of yoga to become a certified teacher. It was during her training that she was introduced to another teacher who was a Certified Sound Practitioner. This teacher talked about the importance of sound in yoga.

After taking several masterclasses with this teacher, she called me and excitedly said, "Mom! This man talks just like you! He does things like you do, but he's playing instruments I've never seen before."

After her graduation, she remained friends with this particular teacher and invited me to come to New York and experience one of his Sound Bath Experiences. Sound Baths/ Sound Experiences are a fully immersive, full body experience that invites healing, therapy, and pause to restore your body and mind. These Sound Bath sessions include many unique types of instruments, including singing bowls, flutes, harps, gongs, and a stringed instrument called a monchord. The sessions are filled with free-flowing compositions, and participants are invited to experience the sounds with their eyes covered to reduce outside stimuli.

That's when my world changed.

During this immersive and moving session, many things clicked with me and I had what some people would call an awakening. For the first time I realized that the love of music, sound, and modalities that had filled my life since childhood were not a side benefit. It was something I could use to help heal myself and help others heal as well. As much joy as I got from creating mixtapes for patients, I was never allowed to experience their process with them or even ask self-inquiry questions. I couldn't be with them to create a safe space while they reaped the benefits of sound therapy.

What I learned that day took my life in a whole new direction. I felt like Sound Therapy was something I'd been training for my whole life. It was a new and powerful modality that I could use to really impact people in the most positive of ways.

After more than two years' extensive and intensive studies with some of the most experienced sound teachers in the world, I'm currently creating a healing community in Santa Fe, New Mexico.

BENEFITS OF SOUND

Like I mentioned previously, vibration touches every part of the body, which means that, if we believe that sound is a vibration and that it touches every part of our body, it also means that our bodies are listening at a much deeper level than we are aware of.

Sound is also a way to hold space for others; it allows us to create a space for rest, peace, and healing for ourselves and others. It works to tune out our chattering minds and helps us deeply connect to our bodies. So much of our time is spent dealing with the endless chatter in our brains, but music (in any form) can help us to "get out of our heads" and let go of worry, guilt, gossip, fear, and judgement.

Sound can help our bodies dispel negative energies that we may have been unconsciously holding on to for years. Moving this negative energy out leaves room for healing to come in.

When we listen to sound, our breathing gets slower, our stress hormones reduce, the immune systems jumps into action, our blood pressure gets slower, and we activate the centers of the brain that release natural opiates to help us feel good.

SOME THOUGHTS ON FREQUENCYISM

We experience sound in the present moment. Sound and its vibrations unhook the mind and the frontal lobe so we can settle into the sound session and fully connect to the present moment. There is something called Frequencyism, as well, that needs to be noted as part of your Practice.

Our bodies are composed of energy centers. In India and parts of Asia these are known as chakras. Where this gets kattywampus is that many energy workers and healers claim that each energy center has its own vibration which can be measured to a specific frequency, called a hertz. So if a healer uses specific "hertz" in their practice, such as a 432 hertz for the heart chakra, that it will cure whatever ails the heart. The truth is that 432 hertz is really just the musical note G. If I knew that the musical note G could cure heart ailments, I would be playing it over and over again 24 hours a day.

In reality, sound is perception. Vibrations are perception. We can hear 432 hertz and perceive it differently at different times of the day, week, or month. Each person experiences sound in a way that is unique to them and not at a specific frequency.

You can be in a room of a hundred people or even 800 people, and every single person will ultimately experience sound in a unique way. Sound is based on individual perception, which is activated in the neurological areas of our brains. It's based on the physiology of our inner ear, how we perceive our surroundings, plus what has happened to us that day and throughout life.

My beliefs are that, yes, sound should be part of your self-healing process, but in my experience Frequencyism is not a "thing." Sound is based on perception and is based on the physiology of our inner ear. If I give you "432 hertz" of sound in the morning to "open your heart chakra," it may be a lovely and beneficial experience. But if I give that same experience to the same person at 5:30 at night when the phone is ringing and the kids are crying, that same sound will not be perceived in the same way, thus the experience will be completely different.

Sound is a perception and is not prescriptive by tone and frequency. Because I am sharing this belief with you, I know I will not be well received with many of these thought leaders. But science backs me on this.

SOUND HEALING INSTRUMENTS

Sound healing instruments are thousands of years old in their origin, and the instruments that I play during my healing sessions are rooted in century-old traditions. One of my favorite ancient instruments is a kantele. A kantele or kannel is a traditional Finnish, Karelian instrument and is a five, ten, or eleven string harp that is played as it lays on your lap. Kanteles also come in concert versions that have a switch mechanism (similar to semitone levers on a modern folk harp) for making sharps and flats. I prefer to use the 5-11 string harps that are in alignment with my Nordic/Scandinavian heritage.

Sound healing instruments are very different from common instruments like piano and guitar, which are considered tempered instruments. Tempered instruments have certain scales and a specific way of being tuned, and that is how they are played. Healing instruments are considered non-tempered instruments. Examples of non-tempered instruments include a monochord harp, singing bowls, gongs, tuning forks, and kanteles. Himalayan Singing Bowls are considered "alive" for up to 300 years. After 300 years, they disintegrate. Made of a bronze composite metal, they were originally created to put food in, and they come in many sizes.

The common thread is that sound healing instruments play one fundamental note but include an overtone series. That overtone series follows the Fibonacci Sequence.

The Fibonacci sequence is a series of numbers where a number is the addition of the last two numbers, starting with 0 and 1.

The Fibonacci Sequence: 0, 1, 1, 2, 3, 5, 8, 13, 21, 34, 55...

Coming from ancient and classical mathematics, the Fibonacci Sequence is considered sacred geometry and sacred mathematics. Healing sound instruments have an overtones series, 17-21 notes, all of which work to still the mind. They work to "unhook" our frontal lobe so we can get into our parasympathetic nervous system, as opposed to the sympathetic nervous system that is connected to our "fight or flight" mode.

There are people who react negatively to some overtone sounds. For some reason, some people experience discomfort when they are opposed to the sounds of a gong, and even the singing bowls because they are made from gong metal. When this happens, I teach and encourage something called Deep Listening. Deep Listening is the act of accepting all sounds in your container.

DEEP LISTENING

Hearing is one's physiological ability to perceive sound and receive vibration that doesn't require any action from us. *Listening* is a conscious act of the brain that understands and analyzes the sounds that we are hearing, and concentration is required.

During my Sound Therapy Sessions, I teach something called Deep Listening, a term coined by American composer Pauline Oliveros. This is the act of accepting all of the sounds in our current environment without letting it dictate what direction our minds will go. I refer to our immediate surroundings as a "container," and deep listening is the choice of acknowledging the sounds in our container without choosing to fixate on it. There are ways to invoke deep listening, and the first step is to get silent. In that silence, we can concentrate and observe all of the sounds around us. To take that listening even deeper, we appreciate each and every sound. This gets us out of our heads and down into our bodies. This deep appreciation is also part of our Gratitude Practice.

As I work on this chapter, the garbage truck is pulling up outside, and I know the roar of the engine will be followed by the scraping and banging of the plastic garbage cans. I can't physically "unhear" these distractions, but I can choose to accept it as a sound in my container with awareness and no judgement.

When we try to listen normally, we will automatically bring with us our own set of values, beliefs, and expectations. But, when we use Deep Listening practices, the mind shifts, and our mind truly starts listening to the sounds instead of the chatter in our heads. The more we listen deeply, the more we hear. The more we hear, the more we understand that we are part of an inclusive and expansive universe.

This new revelation translates to our outside world and everyday life as well. The more we practice Deep Listening, the more we are working to increase our empathy and understanding for others because we listen deeply and closely. We also hear the things that aren't being said. Deep Listening is also useful in a workplace setting, because it helps teams understand that everything matters.

Sound creates the appropriate and optimal conditions for natural healing in the body and helps you connect more deeply to the people around you. Through the use and journey through sound, you can understand your personal relationship with sound and your environment.

Every cell in our body responds to sound, which is further proof that we "listen" with more than our ears. Listening is not an unconscious act; concentration is required. In order to invoke deep listening, we need to shut off our own personal dialogue that tends to be on repeat in our minds.

As you move forward in this journey, my hope for you is that you will learn the art and practice of deep listening and the way you listen to the world around you and use it as a point of self-inquiry.

To create a sound practice in your life, I invite you to look at the Mongata Healing Center site **mongata.org**, as well as our social media on Facebook, Instagram, and YouTube. I'm creating sound mediation downloads and live streaming events weekly and monthly. There are also some really great apps out there that do the same thing. A few of my favorites are Calm, Insight Timer, and Inscape.

MOVEMENT

I came to Movement as a healing modality entirely by accident. While many of you and others in my life have been running marathons, weightlifting, doing yoga, etc., I've spent the last 20+ years walking four miles daily.

Until, that is, I found myself significantly injured to the point I couldn't do my walking practice anymore. I had to pause and place both feet on each step when going up and downstairs. My swollen and painful knees wouldn't bend and would throb day and night. Even turning over in bed became a major event. Listen, I was no athlete, but I did lead an active life traveling, raising kids, and moving around a lot each day.

Instinctively I sat down and did little so I could nurture my injured body. I put on ice packs, then heat packs. I rested, but I didn't take anti-inflammatory medication because I know the secondary issues associated with them, such as liver and kidney disease. I knew this was a chronic issue and did my best to bring down the swelling so that the pain would go away.

The pain was becoming so great that I could barely hold my body weight.

"I'm just standing here," I remember thinking to myself in frustration. "I'm not even moving, and everything is hurting. This isn't normal!"

There were days when all I could do was sit and feel the extreme and exceptional pain in my body. Tears just rolled down my eyes. It reminded me of giving birth to my children. You have only one choice, and that is to surrender to it.

There was this moment when giving birth to my first child when I thought, "I can't do this. I really can't do this. I can't bear to linger in this agonizing pain one minute more."

From my mind's perspective, I wanted to contract or flee. My body was going through its natural process of giving life, but my mind couldn't wrap itself around what was happening.

I came to this space, and something shifted inside my mind. I knew that the only way I would get to the other side of this pain was to **open into** the agony of my pain. I need to focus on the other side of it, not that moment.

I remembered this lesson from long ago as the days ticked by and my aching knees continued to hinder me. Here I was in my 50s, with my body wanting to shut down, and the toll it was taking on my spirit was indescribable. When our bodies are not working optimally, it affects our emotional and mental well-being as well.

Not being able to be my active self (and social self, because we were in the throes of a global pandemic) was more debilitating than I could have ever imagined. This was not what my life plan was supposed to look like!

With a bit of glib in my voice and a smile on my face, I would tell people that I'm known as Vallie the Viking and that's an earned name, meaning that if pushed into a corner I will fight my way out and I won't be taking any hostages. Now my body had put me in a corner, and I was going to have to fight the long, hard fight to get myself out. There were no hostages to take.

I knew I was either going to be a victim or I was going to heal and get some semblance of my life back.

It's always been my goal to age vibrantly, but this dark time in my life was the exact opposite of this. Soon, I began to doubt myself and mentally swirl into a dark cavern of uncertain worries. Was I on a slippery slope? Or was there a way back to wholeness?

As I mentioned earlier, you need to start where you are at that very moment to proceed and improve. I could spend hours and days mourning the loss of my mobility, or I could choose to laser focus on making improvements to each second of my day. Once my mindset shifted from defeat to my Vallie the Viking fighting spirit, the sun began to peek through my cloud of pain and despair.

Through my body, I opened through the pain. I acknowledged it. I recognized it. I called it what it was. This included my emotional and mental pain as well. I opened up through the heartache, through the longing, through the disappointment, and focused on the other side of it all.

I focused on light and healing. And my first step was to ask for help.

My Integrative physician in Santa Fe put me on anti-inflammatory teas and encouraged me to increase my water intake drastically. These homeopathic practices had an immediate effect on my discomfort level, and the swelling in my joints began to recede within a few days. Around the same time, I was scrolling through Instagram, and Sara Colquhoun popped up in my feed. I had never heard of her, but there she was!

When the student is ready, the teacher will appear.

Sara Colquhoun, a Pilates instructor from Australia, was in lockdown like the rest of the world. Unable to hold in-person classes, she did the next best thing and began doing this straightforward exercise in her kitchen and sharing them on Instagram. At that moment, the light bulb went on in my head, and I was mesmerized by her energy and teachings.

One of her recommended activities consisted of standing with a foot on a kitchen dish towel, moving it back and forth behind her. Then she repeated this move, but to the side.

"I can do that," I remember thinking. So, I did. I got up and did it on both legs three times, holding onto a kitchen counter on either side of me.

The next day I did it again and then scrolled on her feed to list the exercises I could do. Each day's movement consisted of repeating these moves, and each day, she would post new things to do. Before too long, I was moving for 30 minutes each day.

I repeated these standing exercises day after day, and soon my body, my swelling, and my joints began showing a better range of motion. A little over two months later, I splurged and bought myself a Pilates Bolster so I could graduate from doing the exercises standing to being able to do them without getting down on the floor.

By the end of the summer, I was walking three miles every other day.

Here's what I learned from all of this:

Our bodies want to move.

My body wants to move.

Your body wants to move.

Our bodies are designed to stay strong and vital, as well as pain-free, throughout our entire lives, regardless of how old we are or how old we're going to be.

Our bodies are programmed to continually heal and repair themselves after damage or an injury has happened. Whether we are recovering from broken bones, torn muscles, cuts, burns, or fighting off germs and bacteria, our body's primary objective is to heal.

The more you move, the more you charge and fuel the remarkable cells in your body to meet these challenges with a healing response.

Your body is a complex system created by other complex systems to keep you vibrant and active into extreme old age. Our fountain of youth doesn't exist in our minds, hearts, or lungs but is fueled by the muscle system. When our muscles are strong, we feel less pain and have better circulation; it lowers blood sugar and increases our energy, giving us better focus, stronger memory, and sharper thinking.

When our brains create more brain cells, it brings more oxygen into our bodies.

Movement in the body also lowers cholesterol, improves our cardiovascular health, and slashes the risk of type 2 diabetes, cancer, Alzheimer's disease, high blood pressure, and other chronic illnesses.

I'm happy to report that Sara's simple baby steps in my kitchen have now led me to embrace Movement wholly. I have become a certified Qigong practitioner and continue to study women's Qigong. I still walk daily, and I do Pilates with Sara over at the Sweat Community. The most important part of all these practices is that I listen deeply to my body and what it is teaching me and communicating.

My body wants to move. It still wants to move. Your body wants to move too. Let's move and heal.

Want to know where to begin with your movement practice? Start small and work up to bigger things. My favorite movement practice is walking. Do what you can. When my knees were so swollen that I couldn't bend them, and I learned I had to get back moving again, I started by walking to the front gate and back. Then I extended it out to the corner, each day extending it out a little further until I was back to walking.

Another movement practice I love a lot is Pilates. The Pilates machines are still very challenging for me, but I greatly enjoy doing Pilates mat workouts. I work out with Sara on the Sweat app. Other apps that have really nice mat Pilates workouts are Pilates Anytime and Openfit.

If your joints and body movements are feeling stiff, and the hard workouts of yesterday are long gone, I highly recommend Essentrics. These are 30-minute stretching workouts that literally reverse aging and have us moving easily and securely again. Miranda Esmonde White has developed this system over the last 20+ years. Love her workouts!

Another favorite healing exercise system is Qigong. I have studied Qigong for many years now. Daisy Lee is one of my favorites. She teaches traditional medical Qigong but also Tibetan Qigong for Women. I also highly recommend Yoqi on Youtube or her subscription site on her website. Master Mingtong Gu at the Chi Center just outside of Santa Fe is amazing and helped calm my nervous system. Master Mingtong has a beautiful community which meets online and off.

Any type of movement which matches the breath with the movement is incredibly healing for the body. Yoga is the long time go-to for such healing movement. There are so many incredible yoga instructors. Donna Farhi and Tias Little are two of my favorites. Both have online live and stream classes. Please check the resource section for a great selection of different movement classes and methods.

MEDITATION

One of the biggest myths of meditation is that you need to clear your mind completely and block any and all outside distractions. Not only is this hard to do, you likely will end up frustrated and headachy!

Instead, we want to become aware of what our brain is thinking without getting attached to it, without judging anything that comes to mind. Thoughts are also just a part of the container we're living in.

There are many types of meditation techniques, but the one I'd like to focus on is Mindfulness Meditation. Mindfulness Meditation works with any modality you are practicing and also works on its own. This type of meditation has deep ties to Eastern Culture and is deeply rooted in Buddhism. This form was created into its own modality by Jon Kabatt-Zinn. Dr. Kabat-Zinn is an American professor emeritus of medicine and the creator of the Stress Reduction Clinic and the Center for Mindfulness in Medicine, Health Care, and Society at the University of Massachusetts Medical School.

Mindfulness is a type of meditation in which you focus on being intensely aware of what you're sensing and feeling in the moment, without interpretation or judgment. Practicing Mindfulness involves breathing methods, guided imagery, and other practices to relax the body and mind and help reduce stress. By definition, mindfulness means "paying attention on purpose." But Mindfulness Meditation is about paying attention on purpose in a way that unhooks our ruminating mind and brings us to a place of acceptance and calm.

There has been a plethora of studies done that show how meditation and Mindfulness profoundly and positively affect our daily lives. These studies validate that these two habits working in tandem replenish and nurture our spiritual, emotional, mental, and physical selves.

In Chapter 4, *Heartfulness and Mindfulness*, we took an in-depth look at what Mindfulness is and how it benefits our overall well-being. Though this word is seemingly attached to everything that many consider "woo-woo," it is (and will always be) a healthy, free, and effective way to be our best selves.

Practicing Mindfulness in a non-judgemental way isn't easy. Our minds like to be in control and "need" to know what is going on around us every waking moment, but what we need to know tends to clutter up our minds. When our focus lingers and we do, in fact, pay attention, it's very hard for our brains to take in our surroundings in a non-judgemental way. Mindfulness Meditation is the purposeful act of letting go as we sink into a state of patience, curiosity, kindness, acceptance, trust, physical stillness, and gratitude.

LET'S BREAK THESE DOWN A BIT:

Patience: We all want progress and better mental awareness to happen, like...yesterday. We live in a "Nano-Second World" where we've become accustomed to getting what we want at lightning speed. However, if our mind isn't trained on how to become patient, and create our daily Practice, we won't be able to fully experience the benefits of Mindfulness Meditation. The best analogy that I can think of is that it will be like picking an apple before it's ripe. The good news is that even the most impatient people can learn to be patient. Developing patience is the act of developing the belief that things will happen as they and we are at peace with that part of the process. Having patience is the ability to enjoy the ride instead of looking for the expressway.

Curiosity: "Mindfulness without Curiosity is impossible." These words are from *A Clinician's Guide to Teaching Mindfulness*, and I couldn't agree more. When we sit in Mindful Meditation, we are in fact tuning in more deeply to our present moment. In order to observe and learn from these moments, we must be willing to spend some time examining what we are feeling and thinking as a means of deeper exploration of self. We can even take this act one step further and mentally ask ourselves curiosity-based questions like, "Why am I feeling restless right now?"

Kindness: Kindness for others makes the world a better place. Kindness for ourselves helps us to develop a deeper understanding of what makes us tick and how we are all perfectly made. Instead of becoming angry or frustrated at the things we perceive as our shortcomings, we instead see our humanness in a different, and kinder, light.

Acceptance (Non-Judgement): To come from a place of reflection without judgement takes practice. Our brains love to process and overthink. It's like a movie in our minds set to repeat. The beauty of Mindfulness Meditation is not to turn off that constant rhetoric, but to observe and see the effects of these thoughts instead.

Trust (Letting Go/Letting Be): As I've mentioned many times throughout this book, we cannot feel trust until we feel safe. Let's use the analogy of holding a pen. Let's say you have a really tight grip on a pen with your hand locked tightly around it. If I ask you to let go and drop the pen, it means you have to use all of this energy to force your hand open and let the pen drop. If these are your emotions and trauma triggers, this can be a daunting and terrifying idea to just let everything go. But let's look at it another way. You still have a tight grip on that pen, but now turn your hand over so that when you open the hand, the pen is just sitting there. That is an open container where you can see and observe anything and everything in it. You can move these emotions and trauma with your breath, movement, meditation, sound practices, or all of the above. The emotions and trauma release up and out on its own choosing.

Physical and Mental Stillness: Many of us are just not feeling right with the world unless we are striving for something more. This can be both a blessing and a curse. The blessing is that we have the hustle, drive, and follow-through that help make our dreams come true. The curse is that we don't work to turn our brains off so we can become one with peace and stillness. Our bodies and minds desperately need these times of rejuvenation and replenishment, so we don't find ourselves in a state of burnout and overwhelm.

Gratitude: The act of gratitude is one of the most powerful ways to connect with Source energy. When you are thankful for something, that usually means that it's already happened. Gratitude is when you are in a state of appreciation. When you are appreciating something, like when you are outside enjoying nature, it means you are connected to Life Source Energy. Even if what you are manifesting and co-creating hasn't appeared in your life yet, if you are in a state of gratitude as if it has already appeared in your life, synchronicities will occur that help you produce this in your life. This thankfulness and gratitude mindset has been proven in quantum physics and neuroscience to be a powerful way to manifest the things in life that we all deserve.

THE COMPONENTS TO MINDFULNESS MEDITATION

There are three main components to Mindfulness Meditation, and this simplicity is one of the many reasons I love it so much for my own Practice. These components include:

- An intention to cultivate awareness (and return to it again and again)

- Paying attention to what is occurring in the present moment (simply observing thoughts, feelings, sensations as they arise)

- Cultivating an attitude of non-judgemental, curious, and kind thoughts and behavior

Some people have asked me what the difference is between regular meditation and Mindfulness Meditation. Mindfulness Meditation is the awareness of "some-thing," while meditation is the awareness of "no-thing."

HOME PRACTICE

Choosing how and when you are going to practice Mindfulness is just as important as the actual session itself. A lot of people prefer to do this at home because they can carve out a little corner in their house specifically for practicing.

Again, Mindfulness can be done at any time or any place. Choosing your specific place is entirely up to you. The place you choose is where you most likely feel the least distracted.

When you practice, you might want to use the same position all the time to allow for continuity. There are several you can choose from so let's cover a few here:

During Activities: Even though you are busy during the day (be it at home or work), give yourself time to stop, breathe, and notice your surroundings. You can basically be doing anything as long as you take the time to genuinely stop and become mindful.

Walking: If you are on a walk, notice everything around you. Notice the birds, the clouds, the trees, the children playing in the park, the colors of buildings or houses, the animals. Walk so that your arms are swaying back and forth freely (front to back), you are walking tall, eyes looking all around, and your body is relaxed.

Sitting: Sit in a chair with your back straight (if you are able), and keep your hands sitting on your legs with your palms up and your feet flat on the floor.

Lying down: Lie flat on the floor without crossing your legs or your arms. Allow your hands to fall beside you, again with your palms up. For comfort, you can put a pillow under your head or knees.

Yoga Position: Sit with your legs crossed and your hands resting gently on your knees. This is similar to the pose used in yoga and other forms of meditation.

Finding time to practice Mindfulness is probably something you think you don't have time for in your busy, hectic day. It only takes 10-15 minutes at the same time every day. Try to do it first thing in the morning, mid-day or before you go to bed. And, don't forget to journal about your entire Mindfulness session in order to keep track of your thoughts, feelings, and actions during your session. When you look back at your journal entries you will see how your entire healing journey unfolded. You will be amazed at how far you have come and how powerful you are.

APPROACHING MINDFULNESS MEDITATION WITH A BEGINNER'S MIND

Not only are many of us toting around an overthinking mind, we have intelligent brains that are naturally wired to always be looking to do things "better." My advice to you, when creating your Mindfulness Meditation Practice as part of your Four Pillars, is to approach it with a beginner's mind.

When we are new at something, we tend to pay rapt attention to the instructions we are given. Mainly because of curiosity, but there's also a layer of fear in there that we won't "get it right." When nurturing your Practice, let all of that go and just be in the moment with no judgement, fear, or ego. Children have this "all in" laser-like-focus attention down pat when they are learning something new. But as adults, our ruminating mind is always questioning and second-guessing what we are about to do. Turn all of that OFF!

A beginner's mindset allows us all to see something as fresh, new, and full of possibilities. We set an intention to enter this new Mindful Meditation Practice with fresh eyes and an open mind. A beginner's mind also invites a sense of wonder and awe to fill our space and time. We tend to lose our sense of wonderstruck when we are going through the motions of something based on the fact that we've done it a million times. Treat your Mindfulness Meditation Practice with the same fresh reverence that children do when they see a kite fly for the first time or experience the feeling of holding their baby brother or sister for the first time.

Out with the judgement and bias. Instead, welcome in the newness of an experience that has no strings attached.

A Mindfulness Meditation Practice can be adapted to any age, mobility, or level of experience and it can also be practiced alone or as part of a larger group.

Mindfulness is not the end-all cure, but it can help alleviate symptoms that drugs or pills can't touch. You and your mind are in control of your body, so you need to think outside of the box and use other techniques that you can control and do on your own. By getting your mind in a healthy place, it can only enhance the medical help you are receiving.

One or all Four Pillars of Breath, Sound, Movement, and Meditation are a great beginning to getting in touch with yourself. It brings our mind and body together in unison, giving us the tools to observe and process life's traumas and illnesses to bring us to a place of centeredness, rest, and calm. These Pillars unhook our oftentimes overactive and ruminating minds, help us see where we are holding our stress and trauma in our bodies, and help us shift them out so that we may return to our original state of wholeness. I truly hope you enjoy exploring these wonderful self-healing experiences and discovering how they can help your heart sing.

CHAPTER 8
INTEGRATION

"Try new things and discover yourself every single day."

– BHAVYA CHOUDHARY

Congratulations! You are now armed with the tools you need to begin (and continue) this journey of Health & Well-Being Empowerment through the practice of Self-Care, Inner Peace, and Renewal!

Now for the next, and incredibly important, step: Integrating all you've learned into a lifelong practice that will nurture and facilitate self-healing. As intelligent human beings, we love information and wisdom that will help us live better lives. The problem for many is that, though our intentions are good, our follow-through is not. Now is the time to commit to a shift in perspective and to create a plan of action that will help you continue to move forward, grow and bloom.

The past only equals the future if you decide to live there. From this day on, the past will no longer define your future, and together we will choose to embrace the present moment that we're living in. Today, we get to choose what stories we're going to create, and we do that in this very present moment.

Let's begin the Integration of all that you have learned so far.

WHAT IS INTEGRATION

Integration is being fully aware of when you need to move negative energy out so that it no longer robs you of your freedom.

Integration is about not only being aware of what triggers you but also putting a name to it.

Integration is acknowledging that to heal from our emotions, we need to feel them.

"Navigate life's stresses like a bamboo in the wind. When tension (the wind) rises, you can bend with it, but you will always come back to center because your roots are deep and strong."

– VALARIE BUDAYR

Integration is turning to one of the Four Pillars (or all of them!) to show up for life instead of shutting down. With the new Body Wisdom you have gained, paired with the tools you have learned about in *Thrive*, you will be able to move through these triggering moments by putting all of the concepts and modalities in this book to use.

And you will be able to live from a place of freedom instead of limitations.

NEXT STEPS AND WHAT THAT MEANS

As you welcome this new "neck down" way of listening to the wisdom of your body, you will also be shifting away from passing over, or covering up, what has been weighing you down mentally, physically, emotionally, and spiritually for a very long time.

This means that, as you do your Breathwork, Sound Practice, Meditation, and Movement Practice, you will notice how much better you feel. One of the first steps in integrating your newfound self-healing journey is to ask yourself, "How can I continue to live from this place."

This is when everything changes.

We use our imaginations to make our thoughts and visualizations more real than anything else, thereby creating a thriving new reality.

To achieve this, we're going to start by collecting evidence of why we are so entirely trustworthy and why our intuitions are always guiding us, to reveal how we already have clear direction when we ask for it and how we will benefit when we choose to follow it. To embody trust in our minds and hearts, we will work to release the old stories and conditioning that have been keeping us in a State of Stuck for far too long.

CREATING RITUAL AND ROUTINES

When you are integrating your new Practice into your daily routine, you may have enthusiastic ideas that require more time and attention than you currently have. If you have the time and space to create a robust Practice, I say, "Go for it!"

But the majority of us are managing lives filled with mothering, working, family commitments, and other demands on our already stretched thin days. I encourage everyone to start slow and make small (but significant) changes to begin their Practice of Self-Healing.

My advice is to "meet yourself where you are." If your new practice looks like 10 minutes a day, that is Enough. Like I mentioned in Chapter 6, in order to create this new way of Being, we need to begin **right here**. We need to begin practice **where we are right now**.

Your Practice doesn't have to be perfect, pretty, grandiose, or expensive. It just needs to suit *you*.

If your Right Now, Right Here Practice consists of you working on your self-healing journey alone, that is perfectly fine. That is Enough.

If it looks like working on your Practice in a studio with other like-minded students of self-healing, that is perfectly fine as well. That is also Enough.

Peeling away what no longer serves you takes time, patience, and commitment as well. But it is so worth it.

THE PEELING OF YOUR ONION

Every December, I find myself pausing, looking back, and reflecting on the months that have since passed. Not surprisingly, my 2020 annual review was like no other. In previous years, I'd comb through the months gone by, make a list of my accomplishments in a well-crafted newsletter or blog post, and then proceed to start letting the year go and prepare myself for the new one to follow. My pre-New Year prep always included choosing a Word of The Year. Just ONE WORD that will be my theme as I create my aspirations over the next 12 months.

But since 2020 was such a challenging year for all of us, the constant extreme of highs and lows didn't feel healthy to recap in my "well-crafted newsletter." Over the course of 2020, everything had changed, and it felt more like I was focusing on surviving instead of thriving.

And I know I wasn't the only one.

In the throes of a global pandemic and global chaos, I didn't even want to pick a new word for the next year. One solitary word felt like such an effort for my already muddled brain.

The subject of picking One Word came up again closer to the dawn of 2021 as I was talking with my friend Becky. A true advocate for picking One Word that would act as a guiding light for the coming year, she revealed to me that she had chosen TWO words for 2021. One to share and one for her and only her.

She then shared that she secretly chose the word "onion" for her word of 2021. "Onion" was poignant for her because it represented the peeling back of layers that no longer served her to reach the strong core of who she really was. The moment I heard her Word of the Year, it completely resonated with me, but I wasn't sure why at that moment.

At first, I used it as a joke. My 2021 Word of the Year wouldn't be about the year to come, instead it was about the year that was. All I could think about was that onions produce painful tears while cooking and that was a great reflection of 2020 for many of us.

I mentioned my "Onion" Word of the Year with glib cuteness to a couple of my friends here in New Mexico and received clarity to the question of why it had resonated with me, which had been lurking in the back of my mind.

They LOVED my word and said that their families and/or communities would gather women together to cut onions so that they could cry with purpose all the while preparing something good to eat at the end. What started as a joke unfolded into a sacred journey.

They also shared that the onion is intimately known in both myth and symbolism for the magic of its tears. I see this all around me in the cultures of New Mexico. They have not only incorporated onion into their delicious cooking but they have embraced her as a way of releasing both privately and in the community.

So, why am I telling you this story? Because, as you create your own Self-Healing Journey, you will feel like the magical onion. You also will be peeling away the layers that no longer are needed to get to the core of your Very Best You. Your journey to healing and self-awareness will likely have a few tears and rotten parts, but those will pass to reveal a new layer of You that you had forgotten about.

Or have never had the chance to meet.

This is your time, and you will be the hero of your own story. Taking the first step and buying (and reading!) *Thrive: Living a Self-Healed Life* was huge. And now it's up to you to keep the momentum forward to a better way of living.

Like I've mentioned before, you are not alone. I'm here and I know there will be other people in your life who will fall into step beside you as you traverse this new road to wellness.

You are your own best medicine. Every student who comes to Mongata's in-person classes, participates in one of my many upcoming online courses, or simply shows up daily with a renewed commitment to creating a better life, will be the heroes of their own story

Creating your routines and rituals for self-healing is a very personal experience and unique to each of us. If you find yourself wanting a little support in getting started, I welcome you to join the Mongata Healing community with one of our on-demand classes or upcoming online courses. I've designed Thrive: An 8-Week Pathway to Healing & Living Vibrantly, a course just for you. You can find the sign-up at **www.mongata.org**, and it's also listed in the resource section. I also offer 1:1 mentoring and coaching for your healing path.

It's time to **#livevibrantly**. At Mongata Healing Center, we believe in empowering you with the tools you need to self-heal. Our goal is always to Live Vibrantly. Please join our community and share the moments of your self-healing journey with us by using the hashtag #LiveVibrantly. It's been a pleasure to start this journey with you, and I am so excited for us to continue on and Thrive together.

Much love,

Valarie

ABOUT THE AUTHOR

VALARIE BUDAYR is a Board-Certified Sound and Breath Practitioner and Mindfulness Teacher who guides others towards self-discovery and self-healing with the principles of sound, movement, breath, a connection with nature, inner traditions, depth psychology, and wisdom practices.

She is an author, publisher, and CEO of AudreyPress.com, seeker, warrior, Wise Woman, and Founder of Mongata, an online and offline center for well-being and inner healing. As the daughter of immigrant parents, her Gotland, Sweden ancestral roots and heritage strongly influence her beliefs, values, practices, and desire to express kindness and inclusion for all.

Through Practice Leadership, Valarie teaches others to use transformational tools to reinforce the Knowing that we are all our own best medicine that will help them improve and heal their mind, body, and spirit. Valarie invites her students and clients into immersive explorations of the self through Mongata's in-person classes, online courses, daily meditation practices, and the wisdom shared on her ValarieBudayr.com website.

Her life mission is to share the beauty and wonder of the world while empowering others to be their best selves and show up daily with a renewed commitment to creating a better life so they can be the heroes of their own story.

ABOUT MONGATA INNER HEALING CENTER

Mongata Inner Healing Center is a well-being and inner healing community that guides participants on a personal journey from surviving to thriving. Fostering a continuous journey of self-healing, Mongata helps individuals and families work to heal from past trauma, manage daily triggers, and ultimately live vibrantly. Using Practices like Sound, Breath, Movement, and Meditation, our community works to curate beauty and wholeness to create a better world for all.

Mongata is also a curated space for you to come to your own well-being and deepened senses. Through the tools and Practices of Breath, Sound, Movement, and Meditation, you will discover the alignment and inner healing needed to create a life that is vibrant and whole.

A Mongata Practice is about fully coming into ourselves and our energies and our expert-guided classes, courses, and one-on-one sessions are accessible to everyone. Mongata is a safe place where you can give yourself permission to feel all of your emotions and release them while being supported in your healing journey.

Like the phases of the moon, life is constantly changing, and finding a path to help maintain our inner balance, regardless of what life throws our way, has never been more important.

We're here to help you light your path, wherever you may be on your journey to inner healing.

Breathe with us. Move with us. Grow with us.

THRIVE THE ONLINE COURSE

Please look for our foundational course, Thrive, on Mongata. org. Thrive is an 8-week course facilitated by Mongata founder Valarie Budayr that will introduce you to breathwork, sound therapy, movement, meditation, and reflective journaling. These practices will guide and help you reconnect into your body so that you can access your innate wisdom, safety, and calm.

Learn more at **ValarieBudayr.com** or Mongata.org and click "Classes" for details and sign-up information.

SNEAK PEEK AT BOOK TWO IN THE THRIVE SERIES: *PLENTIFUL*

MONEY IS AN INSIDE JOB.

What does that mean? It means that Money is many things, but most importantly, it is *energy*. Suppose you live a life where you are feeling hindered by the weight of financial lack or are even living a "Golden Handcuffs" scenario (your job is high paying, but it sucks your energy). In that case, your financial situation is tied to the energy that has manifested in your life and body.

When we look at Money from a holistic perspective, it is not as much about having a big paycheck or the correct financial planning strategy as learning and practicing Money's Energetics.

Plentiful, by definition, means abundant. Within the pages of *Plentiful: Becoming Worthy, Wealthy, and Wise*, I will address the fact that Money is often holding women back from getting out of toxic jobs and situations. This belief applies to men as well, but the matter of Money REALLY affects women.

From birth, we are all unknowingly groomed to believe that Money is the golden thread that ties us to our self-worth, destiny, and social status in life. It's time to snip that invisible golden thread, ditch the money blocks, and begin living from a place of self-worth. When we feel that we are not enough or not good enough, this also translates to how much Money we have in our bank accounts; we fear and feel that we do not and will never have enough. As adults, we tend to get trapped on the never-ending treadmill of striving for more, which becomes a life-long struggle to get more.

These blocks and the belief that "If I only had money, I could_____" is what keeps us from being abundant in life.

The real key to financial freedom isn't changing our job or what we do but how we feel. Learning how we think about Money and where the blocks are and how to heal them is more profound than learning how to invest and keep a budget.

Plentiful will work topic by topic along with helpful and insightful exercises to get to the root of the problem and do the internal work needed to replace feelings of unworthiness with a healed and stronger sense of one's own personal values.

Within the pages of *Plentiful,* we are going to get REAL about the money issues we face every single day. We will dive deep into the excuses we all use to avoid living and seeing ourselves as worthy of abundance in all its forms.

I know from personal experience that once you take back your financial power, positive and beautiful things start to happen. *Plentiful* will give tools to clear the path for wholeness, fulfillment, and richness in all areas of our lives, not just the totals in our bank accounts.